THE PELICAN SHAKESPEARE
GENERAL EDITOR : ALFRED HARBAGE
AB4
THE WINTER'S TALE

WILLIAM SHAKESPEARE

The
Winter's Tale

EDITED BY BALDWIN MAXWELL

PENGUIN BOOKS
BALTIMORE · MARYLAND

This edition first published 1956
Reprinted 1964, 1966
Penguin Books Inc.
3300 Clipper Mill Road, Baltimore, Maryland 21211

Printed in the United States of America

CONTENTS

SHAKESPEARE AND HIS STAGE

William Shakespeare was christened in Holy Trinity Church, Stratford-on-Avon, April 26, 1564. His birth is traditionally assigned to April 23rd. He was the eldest of four boys and two girls who survived infancy in the family of John Shakespeare, glover and trader of Henley Street, and his wife Mary Arden, daughter of a small landowner of Wilmcote. In 1568 John was elected Bailiff (equivalent to Mayor) of Stratford, having already filled the minor municipal offices. The town maintained for the sons of the burgesses a free school, taught by a university graduate and offering preparation in Latin sufficient for university entrance; its early registers are lost, but there can be little doubt that Shakespeare received the formal part of his education in this school.

On November 27, 1582, a license was issued for the marriage of William Shakespeare (aged eighteen) and Ann Hathaway (aged twenty-six), and on May 26, 1583, their child Susanna was christened in Holy Trinity Church. The inference that the marriage was forced upon the youth is natural but not inevitable; betrothal was legally binding at the time, and was sometimes regarded as conferring conjugal rights. Two additional children of the marriage, the twins Hamnet and Judith, were christened on February 2, 1585. Meanwhile the prosperity of the elder Shakespeares had declined, and William was impelled to seek a career outside Stratford.

The tradition that he spent some time as a country teacher is old but unverifiable. Because of the absence of records his early twenties are called the "lost years," and only one thing about them is certain – that at least some of these years were spent in winning a place in the acting profession. He may have begun as a provincial trouper, but by 1592 he was established in London and prominent enough to be attacked. In a pamphlet of that year, *Groatsworth of Wit*, the ailing Robert Greene complained of the neglect which university writers like himself had suffered from actors, one of whom was daring to set up as a playwright:

> ... an upstart crow beautified with our feathers, that with his *Tiger's heart wrapt in a player's hide* supposes he is as well able to bombast out a blank verse as the best of you, and being an absolute Johannes-factotum, is in his own conceit the only Shake-scene in a country.

The pun on his name, and the parody of his line "O tiger's heart wrapt in a woman's hide" (*III Henry VI*), pointed clearly to Shakespeare. Some of his admirers protested, and Henry Chettle, the editor of Greene's pamphlet, saw fit to apologize:

> I am as sorry as if the original fault had been my fault, because myself have seen his demeanor no less civil than he excellent in the quality he professes. Besides divers of worship have reported his uprightness of dealing, which argues his honesty, and his facetious grace in writing that approves his art. (Prefatory epistle, *Kind Heart's Dream*)

The plague closed the London theatres for many months in 1593-94, denying the actors their livelihood. To this period belong Shakespeare's two narrative poems, *Venus and Adonis* and *Rape of Lucrece*, both dedicated to the Earl

8

of Southampton. No doubt the poet was rewarded with a gift of money as usual in such cases, but he did no further dedicating and we have no reliable information on whether Southampton, or anyone else, became his regular patron. His sonnets, first mentioned in 1598 and published without his consent in 1609, are intimate without being explicitly autobiographical. They seem to commemorate the poet's friendship with an idealized youth, rivalry with a more favored poet, and love affair with a dark mistress; and his bitterness when the mistress betrays him in conjunction with the friend; but it is difficult to decide precisely what the "story" is, impossible to decide whether it is fictional or true. The real distinction of the sonnets, at least of those not purely conventional, rests in the universality of the thoughts and moods they express, and in their poignancy and beauty.

In 1594 was formed the theatrical company known until 1603 as the Lord Chamberlain's Men, thereafter as the King's Men. Its original membership included, besides Shakespeare, the beloved clown Will Kempe and the famous actor Richard Burbage. The company acted in various London theatres and even toured the provinces, but it is chiefly associated in our minds with the Globe Theatre built on the south bank of the Thames in 1599. Shakespeare was an actor and joint owner of this company (and its Globe) through the remainder of his creative years. His plays, written at the average rate of two a year, together with Burbage's acting won it its place of leadership among the London companies.

Individual plays began to appear in print, in editions both honest and piratical, and the publishers became increasingly aware of the value of Shakespeare's name on the title pages. As early as 1598 he was hailed as the leading English dramatist in the *Palladis Tamia* of Francis Meres:

9

As Plautus and Seneca are accounted the best for Comedy and Tragedy among the Latins, so Shakespeare among the English is the most excellent in both kinds for the stage: for Comedy, witness his *Gentlemen of Verona*, his *Errors*, his *Love labors lost*, his *Love labors won [Taming of the Shrew?]*, his *Midsummers night dream*, & his *Merchant of Venice*; for Tragedy, his *Richard the 2*, *Richard the 3*, *Henry the 4*, *King John*, *Titus Andronicus*, and his *Romeo and Juliet*.

The note is valuable, both in indicating Shakespeare's prestige and in helping us to establish a chronology. In the second half of his writing career, history plays gave place to the great tragedies; and farces and light comedies gave place to the problem plays and symbolic romances. In 1623, seven years after his death, his former fellow actors, John Hemming and Henry Condell, cooperated with a group of London printers in bringing out his plays in collected form. The volume is generally known as the First Folio.

Shakespeare had never severed his relations with Stratford. His wife and children may sometimes have shared his London lodgings, but their home was Stratford. His son Hamnet was buried there in 1596, and his daughters Susanna and Judith were married there in 1607 and 1616 respectively. (His father, for whom he had secured a coat of arms and thus the privilege of writing himself gentleman, died in 1601, his mother in 1608.) His considerable earnings in London, as actor-sharer, part owner of the Globe, and playwright, were invested chiefly in Stratford property. In 1597 he purchased for £60 New Place, one of the two most imposing residences in the town. A number of other business transactions, as well as minor episodes in his career, have left documentary records. By 1611 he was in a position to retire, and he seems gradually to have withdrawn from theatrical activity in order to live in Stratford. In March, 1616, he made a will, leaving token bequests to Burbage, Hemming, and Condell, but the bulk of his estate to his family. The most famous feature of the will, the bequest of the second-best bed to his wife, reveals nothing about Shakespeare's marriage; the quaintness of the provision seems commonplace to those familiar with ancient testaments. Shakespeare died April 23, 1616, and was buried in the Stratford church where he had been christened. Within seven years a monument was erected to his memory on the north wall of the chancel. Its portrait bust and the Droeshout engraving on the title page of the First Folio provide the only likenesses with an established claim to authenticity. The best verbal vignette was written by his rival Ben Jonson, the more impressive for being imbedded in a context mainly critical:

> ... I loved the man, and do honor his memory (on this side idolatry) as much as any. He was indeed honest, and of an open and free nature: he had an excellent fancy, brave notions, and gentle expressions. ... (*Timber or Discoveries*, c. 1623–30)

The reader of Shakespeare's plays is aided by a general knowledge of the way in which they were staged. The King's Men acquired a roofed and artificially lighted theatre only toward the close of Shakespeare's career, and then only for winter use. Nearly all his plays were designed for performance in such structures as the Globe — a three-tiered amphitheatre with a large rectangular platform extending to the center of its yard. The plays were staged by daylight, by large casts brilliantly costumed, but with only a minimum of properties, without scenery, and quite possibly without intermissions. There was a rear stage balcony for action "above," and a curtained rear recess for "discoveries" and other special effects, but by far the major portion of any play was enacted upon the projecting platform, with episode following episode in swift succession, and with shifts of time and place signaled the audience only by the momentary clearing of the stage between the episodes. Information about the identity of the characters and, when necessary, about the time and place of the action was incorporated in the dialogue. No additional indications of place have been inserted in the present editions; these are apt to obscure the original fluidity of structure, with the emphasis upon action and speech rather than scenic background. The acting, including that of the youthful apprentices to the profession who performed the parts of women, was highly skillful, with a premium placed upon grace of gesture and beauty of diction. The audiences, a cross section of the general public, commonly numbered a thousand, sometimes more than two thousand. Judged by the type of plays they applauded, these audiences were not only large but also perceptive.

THE TEXTS OF THE PLAYS

About half of Shakespeare's plays appeared in print for the first time in the folio volume of 1623. The others had been published individually, usually in quarto volumes, during his lifetime or in the six years following his death. The copy used by the printers of the quartos varied greatly in merit, sometimes representing Shakespeare's true text, sometimes only a debased version of that text. The copy used by the printers of the folio also varied in merit, but was chosen with care. Since it consisted of the best available manuscripts, or the more acceptable quartos (although frequently in editions other than the first), or of quartos corrected by reference to manuscripts, we have good or reasonably good texts of most of the thirty-seven plays.

In the present series, the plays have been newly edited from quarto or folio texts depending, when a choice offered, upon which is now regarded by bibliographical specialists as the more authoritative. The ideal has been to reproduce the chosen texts with as few alterations as possible, beyond occasional relineation, expansion of abbreviations, and modernization of punctuation and spelling. Emendation is held to a minimum, and such material as has been added, in the way of stage directions and lines supplied by an alternative text, has been enclosed in square brackets.

None of the plays printed in Shakespeare's lifetime were divided into acts and scenes, and the inference is that the author's own manuscripts were not so divided. In the folio collection, some of the plays remained undivided, some were divided into acts, and some were divided into acts and scenes. During the eighteenth century all of the plays were divided into acts and scenes, and in the Cambridge edition of the mid-nineteenth century, from which the influential Globe text derived, this division was more or less regularized and the lines were numbered. Many useful works of reference employ the act-scene-line apparatus established by the Globe text.

Since the act-scene division thus established is obviously convenient, but is of very dubious authority so far as Shakespeare's own structural principles are concerned, or the original manner of staging his plays, a problem is presented to modern editors. In the present series the act-scene division of the Globe text is retained marginally, and may be viewed as a reference aid like the line numbering. A printer's ornament marks the points of division when these points have been determined by a cleared stage indicating a shift of time and place in the action of the play, or when no harm results from the editorial assumption that there is such a shift. However, at those points where the established division is clearly misleading – that is, where continuous action has been split up into separate "scenes" – the ornament is omitted and the distortion corrected. This mechanical expedient seemed the best means of combining utility and accuracy.

The General Editor.

INTRODUCTION

For the story presented in *The Winter's Tale* no more appropriate title could have been chosen. It is a story such as might have been often told to while away a winter's evening, a story to be heard and reheard with ever increasing pleasure, its very improbabilities and even its geographical and historical inaccuracies being not, as often assumed, the defects of carelessness, but charming if not essential characteristics of an old folk tale. It is a story of early sadness but of final joy, a story to send the hearers off to bed content with their lot and more tolerant of their fellow men.

Surviving records attest to a performance at the Globe Theatre witnessed by a Dr. Simon Forman on May 15, 1611, and to a presentation at court some six months later. Though the evidence supplied by these records is alone too indecisive to establish the date of composition as 1610–1611, it is strongly supported by evidence within the play itself. In both theme and tone, both diction and verse, *The Winter's Tale* bears the closest resemblance to *Cymbeline* and *The Tempest*. Like them it treats the theme of alienation and reconciliation, destruction and rebirth, and like them it embraces the improbabilities of romance. The language, elliptical, involved, and crammed with thought, is that of Shakespeare's latest manner; as is also the verse, with no rhyme save in the songs and the chorus to Act IV, with many speeches beginning or ending in the middle of the line, and with a higher percentage than has any other play of lines with weak or unstressed endings.

As was his usual practice, Shakespeare in *The Winter's Tale* chose for dramatization a story which had already demonstrated its wide appeal. His source was *Pandosto: The Triumph of Time,* written in 1588 by Robert Greene, whose deathbed attack upon him in 1592 as one "beautified with our feathers" Shakespeare seems to have calmly ignored. Inasmuch as Greene's euphuistic romance was one of the most widely read stories of the day, it could hardly have been to disguise his use of it that Shakespeare changed the names of all the characters or transferred to Sicilia the action Greene had placed in Bohemia and to Bohemia what Greene had assigned to Sicilia. In general Shakespeare follows Greene's narrative quite closely through the first three acts, although both by presenting only the last day of Polixenes' visit and by freeing Hermione of the imprudent behavior of her prototype he discards the obvious motivation of Leontes' jealousy. In Greene the newborn princess is by the king's order entrusted to destiny in a boat without rudder or sail and is by fortunate winds borne to the coast where she is discovered by the Shepherd; none corresponding to Antigonus is present to be devoured by a bear. Most of the other changes Shakespeare introduces prepare for the radical change he was to make in Act V. He has the king upon his own initiative, rather than upon the queen's entreaty, seek the verdict of Apollo's oracle, thereby presenting Leontes somewhat more sympathetically; and he introduces Paulina to torture the jealous king and to convince us of his sincere repentance. That engaging rogue Autolycus is, as is also the Shepherd's clownish son, wholly Shakespeare's. Indeed, for the greater part of Act IV Greene's narrative is but the starting point for Shakespeare's creative imagination. For the happy "snapper-up of unconsidered trifles" *Pandosto* offers only Capnio, a colorless attendant upon the prince, who provides no comedy and serves only to make ready the ship for the lovers' escape from Bohemia and to force the old Shepherd aboard with the telltale jewels. For the prince's wooing of the supposed shepherdess, related by Greene in his characteristic imitation of current pseudo-Arcadian pastoralism and in the language of *Euphues,* Shakespeare substitutes the delightful sheep-shearing in IV, iv, with its true and charming presentation of rural life, for which he is indebted to Greene for nothing beyond the mention of "a meeting of all the farmers' daughters," held before the prince had spied the supposed shepherdess, at which the whole day was spent "in such homely pastimes as shepherds use." For little, indeed, is Shakespeare indebted in this most beautiful and memorable scene; Polixenes' prototype does not learn of his son's love for the unrecognized princess until they have fled across the sea. In Act V Shakespeare completely changes both the dénouement and the emphasis. In Greene Bellaria (Hermione) is not revivified; Pandosto (Leontes), having thrown Dorastus (Florizel) into prison, conceives a lustful passion for his unrecognized daughter Fawnia (Perdita), and after her identity has been established and the marriage of the lovers celebrated, he is driven to suicide by the recollection that he had betrayed his friend Egistus (Polixenes), brought death to his queen and his son Garinter (Mamillius), and incestuously desired his own daughter.

The Winter's Tale enjoyed considerable popularity during the years following the May 1611 performance witnessed by Dr. Forman. Not only was it acted at court in November of that year, but eighteen months later it was chosen as one of fourteen plays to be presented as part of the festivities honoring the marriage of Princess Elizabeth to the

Elector Palatine. Two later court performances are recorded before King James's death, and the play was declared "liked" when presented before King Charles in January 1634. But *The Winter's Tale* hardly suited the taste of the Restoration or the eighteenth century. The next recorded performance was more than a century later – in 1741. It was perhaps this short but not unsuccessful revival which led to there being written within the following fifteen years no fewer than three alterations which sought to adapt the play to the taste of the eighteenth century. The most successful of the three was that by David Garrick, whose *Florizel and Perdita. A Dramatic Pastoral* replaced Shakespeare's as the stage version throughout the remainder of the century. In it the events of sixteen years before are narrated by Camillo to a lord of Bohemia, where all the scenes are laid; there Paulina with the secreted Hermione has found refuge, and there Leontes, at last repentant, comes to ask forgiveness of Polixenes. By these changes Garrick sought to avoid the transfer of action from Sicilia to Bohemia and back to Sicilia, the lapse of sixteen years between Acts III and IV, and perhaps the absence from the stage for extended periods of certain principal characters. Although Shakespeare's text regained the stage with the opening of the nineteenth century, much of the later criticism of the play may suggest that critics have found it difficult wholly to escape the prejudices inherited from the eighteenth century, for it is only within the past twenty years that any have declared *The Winter's Tale* one of Shakespeare's masterpieces.

Although earlier critics recognized in *The Winter's Tale* "the golden glow of Shakespeare's genius," praised the beauty and the force of many of its speeches, and marvelled at the daring mastery of its verse, perhaps most before the

1930's found as much to lament as they did to praise. Naturally comparing the plays of his last period with the great tragedies which preceded them, they thought they recognized a decline in Shakespeare's seriousness of purpose, a lessened interest as well in dramatic technique as in the portrayal of properly motivated characters in understandable human situations; and to explain the change they offered such suggestions as boredom or exhaustion resulting from prolonged mental strain, or eagerness to capitalize upon the popularity recently achieved by the romantic tragicomedies of Beaumont and Fletcher. They saw in *The Winter's Tale* the characteristic fault of Beaumont and Fletcher, an undue emphasis upon the highly dramatic situation even when it could be secured only by the sacrifice of character and probability. Distressed by the lapse of sixteen years between Acts III and IV, and perhaps ignoring Shakespeare's usual disregard of the unity of time, they declared *The Winter's Tale* a structural failure, an unsuccessful experiment toward the satisfactory structure of dramatized romance achieved only in *The Tempest*.

Most of those who have discussed the play in the past twenty years have seen it in a quite different light. They have reminded us that to the English Renaissance the pastoral was not escape literature, something to be read for entertainment alone, but that, as witnessed by Sir Philip Sidney's *Arcadia,* the intelligent reader was expected to discover there notable images of virtues to be imitated and vices to be shunned. When, therefore, for the plays which closed his career Shakespeare chose to use the material of romance, there is hardly reason to suspect him of being less serious; rather the very improbability and naïveté of the plots should encourage one to expect a serious purpose. The apparent crudity of the dramatic technique – such as the introduction of Father Time to announce the passing of sixteen years, the frequent speeches of Autolycus addressed directly to the audience, the famous exit of Antigonus "pursued by a bear" – should be viewed not as evidence that Shakespeare had become tired or bored or indifferent, but rather as a deliberate and skillful adoption of a technique which, because it was antique and outmoded, artistically became the dramatization of a remote and marvellous tale.

Far from seeking an explanation for an odd decline in Shakespeare's serious purpose, most recent writers on *The Winter's Tale* have accepted Dr. E. M. W. Tillyard's view that the plays of Shakespeare's last period represent a natural development of the interests shown in his tragedies. The full tragic pattern presents three stages – prosperity, destruction, re-creation. Although the emphasis in Shakespeare's tragedies is naturally upon the first two, in most of them there is at the end at least the promise of a new order. In the tragicomedies of his last years his concern is with the final phase of the tragic pattern, Dr. Tillyard thought; in them "the old order is destroyed as thoroughly as in the main group of tragedies, and it is this destruction that altogether separates them from the realm of comedy in general and from Shakespeare's own earlier comedies in particular." While in *The Tempest* emphasis is upon the third stage of the pattern, re-creation, the earlier stages being presented only in retrospect, in *The Winter's Tale* Shakespeare presents the full pattern; after giving a brief glimpse of earlier prosperity and happiness, he presents, with almost equal emphasis, complete destruction and happy re-creation. In it we are to recognize, also, the cycle of the seasons, Perdita identified as Spring, and perhaps the theme of the vegetation myth of Proserpina, which Shakespeare underscores by several references. When Proserpina was abducted from her mother Ceres by Pluto, the earth withered and vegetation ceased; only upon her release from the nether world did her mother's spirits revive and fertility return to the earth.

As spring may follow fall only after the intervention of winter, so can rebirth follow destruction only after a period of gestation, and forgiveness follow sin only after proved and continuing repentance. A complete treatment of the tragic pattern demands, therefore, an extended period. The lapse of sixteen years between the first three acts of *The Winter's Tale,* sin, alienation, destruction, and the last two acts, forgiveness, reconciliation, rebirth, though it may be thought awkward dramatically, is essential to a complete treatment of the theme. *The Tempest,* with attention centered upon the last stage of the pattern, and that presented in a single day, may appear more compact, more unified, and in its avoidance of suffering more in the spirit of comedy, but to the same extent it is farther removed from the great tragedies and is, perhaps, less serious, less moral than is *The Winter's Tale* with its insistence that sin be paid for before it be forgiven. This insistence, however, in no way lessens the happiness in which the play ends. No play by Shakespeare has a happier ending, nor can a happier ending be conceived, for the happiness is earned by the characters, not merely decreed by the poet. Leontes, purified by his suffering, a sinner no more, deserves those greatest of joys, forgiveness and reunion with those he loved. Hermione, by her selfless surrender to the dictate of the oracle, has earned not only her restoration but the return of her long-lost daughter. And the lost one, Perdita, surely one of Shakespeare's most charming characters, of royal blood but of country rearing, because of her natural manners and simple honesty merits her happy future with the adoring Florizel.

As Dr. Simon Forman in his account of the performance of May 1611 makes no mention of the statue scene, it has been thought by some that this happiest of endings represents a later alteration, that in Shakespeare's original version Hermione, like her prototype in Greene, actually died as reported in Act III, and that the final scene at first presented what is now only related, the identification of Perdita. Forman, however, is here, as always, an unsatisfactory reporter; stating only that the queen was by the oracle declared guiltless, he records nothing of either her death or her supposed death. But whether or not the statue scene be a later addition, it is certainly written by Shakespeare throughout and constitutes the proper — one may almost say the necessary — ending, for the return of Hermione not only completes the happiness with which the play ends but, by more closely joining its two parts, gives to the play a unity it would otherwise lack.

University of Iowa   BALDWIN MAXWELL

Note on the text: The only text of *The Winter's Tale* is that of the folio of 1623. It is an excellent text, obviously prepared from clearly written copy. This copy is now believed to have been a transcript made by the scrivener Ralph Crane, perhaps from Shakespeare's own draft. A characteristic of the folio text is the almost complete absence of stage directions and, save in a few instances, the listing at the opening of each scene of all the characters who appear during the scene, generally with no indication of the exact point at which they enter. In the present text, the entries have been split and distributed to what appear to be the proper points. The act-scene division supplied marginally is that of the Globe text (identical, in the case of this play, with that of the folio).

The Winter's Tale

The Names of the Actors

Leontes, *King of Sicilia*
Mamillius, *young Prince of Sicilia*
Camillo
Antigonus
Cleomenes } *four lords of Sicilia*
Dion
Polixenes, *King of Bohemia*
Florizel, *Prince of Bohemia*
Archidamus, *a lord of Bohemia*
Old Shepherd, *reputed father of Perdita*
Clown, *his son*
Autolycus, *a rogue*
[A Mariner]
[A Gaoler]
Hermione, *Queen to Leontes*
Perdita, *daughter to Leontes and Hermione*
Paulina, *wife to Antigonus*
Emilia, *a lady* [attending on Hermione]
[Mopsa
[Dorcas } shepherdesses]
Other Lords and Gentlemen, [Ladies, Officers, and] Servants,
   Shepherds, and Shepherdesses
[Time, as Chorus]

[Scene

Sicilia and Bohemia]

THE WINTER'S TALE

Archidamus. If you shall chance, Camillo, to visit Bohemia
on the like occasion whereon my services are now on
foot, you shall see, as I have said, great difference betwixt
our Bohemia and your Sicilia.

Camillo. I think this coming summer the King of Sicilia 5
means to pay Bohemia the visitation which he justly
owes him.

Archidamus. Wherein our entertainment shall shame us, we
will be justified in our loves; for indeed –

Camillo. Beseech you – 10

Archidamus. Verily, I speak it in the freedom of my knowledge. We cannot with such magnificence – in so rare –
I know not what to say. We will give you sleepy drinks,
that your senses, unintelligent of our insufficience, may,
though they cannot praise us, as little accuse us. 15

Camillo. You pay a great deal too dear for what's given
freely.

Archidamus. Believe me, I speak as my understanding in-
structs me and as mine honesty puts it to utterance.

I, i, 8–9 (Compare the broken sentences in Archidamus' next speech. He
wishes to say here that the love which Polixenes bears Leontes will make
up for Bohemia's inability to equal the magnificent entertainment shown
Polixenes in Sicilia.)

20 *Camillo.* Sicilia cannot show himself over-kind to Bohemia. They were trained together in their childhoods, and there rooted betwixt them then such an affection which cannot choose but branch now. Since their more mature dignities and royal necessities made separation of their society,

25   their encounters, though not personal, have been royally attorneyed with interchange of gifts, letters, loving embassies; that they have seemed to be together, though absent; shook hands, as over a vast; and embraced, as it were, from the ends of opposed winds. The heavens con-

30   tinue their loves!

Archidamus. I think there is not in the world either malice or matter to alter it. You have an unspeakable comfort of your young prince Mamillius. It is a gentleman of the greatest promise that ever came into my note.

35 *Camillo.* I very well agree with you in the hopes of him. It is a gallant child — one that indeed physics the subject, makes old hearts fresh. They that went on crutches ere he was born desire yet their life to see him a man.

Archidamus. Would they else be content to die?

40 *Camillo.* Yes — if there were no other excuse why they should desire to live.

Archidamus. If the king had no son, they would desire to live on crutches till he had one.   *Exeunt.*

I, ii   *Enter Leontes, Hermione, Mamillius, Polixenes, Camillo,*
       [and Attendants].

Polixenes. Nine changes of the watery star hath been
    The shepherd's note since we have left our throne

23 *branch* flourish   26 *attorneyed* performed by proxy   27 *that* so that
I, ii, 1 *watery star* moon   2 *note* observation

Without a burthen. Time as long again
Would be filled up, my brother, with our thanks,
And yet we should, for perpetuity,   5
Go hence in debt. And therefore, like a cipher,
Yet standing in rich place, I multiply
With one 'We thank you' many thousands moe
That go before it.

Leontes.   Stay your thanks a while
And pay them when you part.

Polixenes.   Sir, that's to-morrow.   10
I am questioned by my fears of what may chance
Or breed upon our absence, that may blow
No sneaping winds at home to make us say,
'This is put forth too truly.' Besides, I have stayed
To tire your royalty.

Leontes.   We are tougher, brother,   15
Than you can put us to't.

Polixenes.   No longer stay.

Leontes. One sev'n-night longer.

Polixenes.   Very sooth, to-morrow.

Leontes. We'll part the time between's then, and in that
I'll no gainsaying.

Polixenes.   Press me not, beseech you, so.
There is no tongue that moves, none, none i' th' world,   20
So soon as yours could win me. So it should now
Were there necessity in your request, although
'Twere needful I denied it. My affairs
Do even drag me homeward, which to hinder
Were in your love a whip to me, my stay   25

---

8 *moe* more (Modern English *more* has absorbed both Early English *ma*
'greater in number' and E. E. *mara* 'greater in degree') 11–14 (a difficult
passage; *that may blow* may express a wish or perhaps a purpose, that there
may blow) 13 *sneaping* biting

To you a charge and trouble. To save both,
Farewell, our brother.

Leontes.   Tongue-tied our queen? Speak you.

Hermione. I had thought, sir, to have held my peace until
You had drawn oaths from him not to stay. You, sir,
30 Charge him too coldly. Tell him you are sure
All in Bohemia's well; this satisfaction
The by-gone day proclaimed. Say this to him,
  He's beat from his best ward.

Leontes.   Well said, Hermione.

Hermione. To tell he longs to see his son were strong.
35 But let him say so then, and let him go;
But let him swear so, and he shall not stay,
We'll thwack him hence with distaffs.
Yet of your royal presence I'll adventure
The borrow of a week. When at Bohemia
40 You take my lord, I'll give him my commission
To let him there a month behind the gest
Prefixed for's parting. Yet, good deed, Leontes,
I love thee not a jar o' th' clock behind
What lady she her lord. You'll stay?

Polixenes.   No, madam.

Hermione. Nay, but you will?

45 *Polixenes.*   I may not, verily.

Hermione. Verily?
You put me off with limber vows, but I,
Though you would seek to unsphere the stars with oaths,
Should yet say, 'Sir, no going.' Verily,
50 You shall not go. A lady's 'Verily' is
As potent as a lord's. Will you go yet?

33 *ward* defense 41 *let him* let him remain *gest* place and time of a visit
42 *good deed* indeed 43 *jar* tick 44 *What lady she* any lady 47 *limber* feeble

Force me to keep you as a prisoner,
Not like a guest, so you shall pay your fees
When you depart and save your thanks. How say you?
My prisoner or my guest? By your dread 'Verily,'   55
One of them you shall be.

Polixenes.   Your guest, then, madam.
To be your prisoner should import offending,
Which is for me less easy to commit
Than you to punish.

Hermione.   Not your gaoler, then,
But your kind hostess. Come, I'll question you   60
Of my lord's tricks and yours when you were boys.
You were pretty lordings then?

Polixenes.   We were, fair queen,
Two lads that thought there was no more behind
But such a day to-morrow as to-day,
And to be boy eternal.

Hermione.   Was not my lord   65
The verier wag o' th' two?

Polixenes. We were as twinned lambs that did frisk i' th' sun,
And bleat the one at th' other. What we changed
Was innocence for innocence; we knew not
The doctrine of ill-doing, nor dreamed   70
That any did. Had we pursued that life,
And our weak spirits ne'er been higher reared
With stronger blood, we should have answered heaven
Boldly 'Not guilty,' the imposition cleared
Hereditary ours.

Hermione.   By this we gather   75
You have tripped since.

53 *fees* payments which gaolers usually demanded of prisoners upon their
release 68 *changed* exchanged 74–75 *the imposition . . . ours* freed even
from original sin

Polixenes.   O my most sacred lady,
Temptations have since then been born to's, for
In those unfledged days was my wife a girl;
Your precious self had then not crossed the eyes
Of my young playfellow.

80 *Hermione.*   Grace to boot!
Of this make no conclusion, lest you say
Your queen and I are devils. Yet go on.
The offenses we have made you do we'll answer,
If you first sinned with us and that with us

85 You did continue fault and that you slipped not
With any but with us.

Leontes.   Is he won yet?

Hermione. He'll stay, my lord.

Leontes.   At my request he would not.
Hermione, my dearest, thou never spok'st
To better purpose.

Hermione.   Never?

Leontes.   Never but once.

Hermione. What? Have I twice said well? When was't be-
90   fore?
I prithee tell me. Cram's with praise, and make's
As fat as tame things. One good deed dying tongueless
Slaughters a thousand waiting upon that.
Our praises are our wages. You may ride's

95 With one soft kiss a thousand furlongs ere
With spur we heat an acre. But to the goal.
My last good deed was to entreat his stay.
What was my first? It has an elder sister,

---

80 *Grace to boot* Heaven help me   92–93 *One . . . that* withholding praise
of one good deed discourages a thousand others   96 *heat* race   *to the goal*
to come to the point

Or I mistake you. O, would her name were Grace!
But once before I spoke to the purpose. When?   100
Nay, let me have't; I long.

Leontes.   Why, that was when
Three crabbèd months had soured themselves to
    death
Ere I could make thee open thy white hand
And clap thyself my love. Then didst thou utter
'I am yours for ever.'

Hermione.   'Tis Grace indeed.   105
Why, lo you now, I have spoke to the purpose twice;
The one for ever earned a royal husband,
Th' other for some while a friend.

     [Gives her hand to Polixenes, and they walk apart.]

Leontes.   *[aside]* Too hot, too hot!
To mingle friendship far is mingling bloods.
I have tremor cordis on me. My heart dances,   110
But not for joy, not joy. This entertainment
May a free face put on, derive a liberty
From heartiness, from bounty, fertile bosom,
And well become the agent. 'T may, I grant.
But to be paddling palms and pinching fingers,   115
As now they are, and making practiced smiles
As in a looking-glass, and then to sigh, as 'twere
The mort o' th' deer — O, that is entertainment
My bosom likes not, nor my brows. Mamillius,
Art thou my boy?

Mamillius.   Ay, my good lord.

---

102 *crabbèd* bitter 104 *clap* pledge 111-14 *This . . . agent* Hermione'
gracious entertainment may well become her if it be due to a hospitable
and generous nature 115 *paddling* caressing 118 *mort o' th' deer* hunter's
horn announcing the death of the deer

120 *Leontes.*   I' fecks!
      Why, that's my bawcock. What, hast smutched thy nose?
      They say it is a copy out of mine. Come, captain,
      We must be neat – not neat but cleanly, captain.
      And yet the steer, the heifer, and the calf
125   Are all called neat. – Still virginalling
      Upon his palm? – How now, you wanton calf?
      Art thou my calf?
      Mamillius.   Yes, if you will, my lord.
      Leontes. Thou want'st a rough pash and the shoots that I
          have,
      To be full like me; yet they say we are
130   Almost as like as eggs. Women say so,
      That will say anything. But were they false
      As o'er-dyed blacks, as wind, as waters, false
      As dice are to be wished by one that fixes
      No bourn 'twixt his and mine, yet were it true
135   To say this boy were like me. Come, sir page,
      Look on me with your welkin eye. Sweet villain!
      Most dear'st! my collop! Can thy dam? – may't be? –
      Affection, thy intention stabs the center!
      Thou dost make possible things not so held,
140   Communicat'st with dreams – how can this be? –
      With what's unreal thou coactive art,
      And fellow'st nothing. Then 'tis very credent
      Thou may'st co-join with something; and thou dost,
      And that beyond commission, and I find it,
145   And that to the infection of my brains
      And hardening of my brows.

120 *I' fecks* in faith   121 *bawcock* fine fellow (Fr. *beau coq*)   *smutched*
smudged   125 *neat* (1) cleanly (2) horned cattle   *virginalling* playing (with
fingers)   128 *pash . . . shoots* head . . . horns   132 *o'er-dyed blacks* colored
fabrics dyed black or weakened by too much dyeing   137 *collop* small
portion   138 *intention* intensity

Polixenes.   What means Sicilia?
Hermione. He something seems unsettled.
Polixenes.   How, my lord?
    What cheer? How is't with you, best brother?
Hermione.   You look
    As if you held a brow of much distraction.
    Are you moved, my lord?
Leontes.   No, in good earnest.   150
    How sometimes nature will betray its folly,
    Its tenderness, and make itself a pastime
    To harder bosoms! Looking on the lines
    Of my boy's face, methoughts I did recoil
    Twenty-three years, and saw myself unbreeched,   155
    In my green velvet coat, my dagger muzzled
    Lest it should bite its master and so prove,
    As ornaments oft do, too dangerous.
    How like, methought, I then was to this kernel,
    This squash, this gentleman. Mine honest friend,   160
    Will you take eggs for money?
Mamillius.   No, my lord, I'll fight.
Leontes. You will? Why, happy man be's dole! My
        brother,
    Are you so fond of your young prince as we
    Do seem to be of ours?
Polixenes.   If at home, sir,   165
    He's all my exercise, my mirth, my matter,
    Now my sworn friend and then mine enemy,
    My parasite, my soldier, statesman, all.
    He makes a July's day short as December,

148 *What cheer . . . brother* (Though the folio gives these words to Leontes, most editors assign them to Polixenes. Spoken by Leontes, they may suggest a forced gaiety.)   154 *methoughts* it seemed to me (variant of *methought*)   161 *take . . . money* be imposed upon   162 *dole* lot

And with his varying childness cures in me
Thoughts that would thick my blood.

170 *Leontes.*   So stands this squire
Officed with me. We two will walk, my lord,
And leave you to your graver steps. Hermione,
How thou lov'st us, show in our brother's welcome.
Let what is dear in Sicily be cheap.

175 Next to thyself and my young rover, he's
Apparent to my heart.

Hermione.   If you would seek us,
We are yours i' th' garden. Shall's attend you there?

Leontes. To your own bents dispose you. You'll be found,
Be you beneath the sky. *[aside]* I am angling now,

180 Though you perceive me not how I give line.
Go to, go to!
How she holds up the neb, the bill to him,
And arms her with the boldness of a wife
To her allowing husband!

         [Exeunt Polixenes, Hermione, and Attendants.]
                 Gone already!

185 Inch-thick, knee-deep, o'er head and ears a forked one!
Go play, boy, play. Thy mother plays, and I
Play too, but so disgraced a part, whose issue
Will hiss me to my grave. Contempt and clamor
Will be my knell. Go play, boy, play. There have
    been,

190 Or I am much deceived, cuckolds ere now;
And many a man there is, even at this present,
Now while I speak this, holds his wife by th' arm,
That little thinks she has been sluiced in's absence

---

170 *thick my blood* make me melancholy   176 *Apparent* heir apparent
182 *neb* face   184 *allowing* approving   185 *forked one* horned one (cuckold)
187 *whose issue* the result of which

And his pond fished by his next neighbor, by
Sir Smile, his neighbor. Nay, there's comfort in't   195
Whiles other men have gates and those gates opened,
As mine, against their will. Should all despair
That have revolted wives, the tenth of mankind
Would hang themselves. Physic for't there's none.
It is a bawdy planet, that will strike   200
Where 'tis predominant; and 'tis powerful, think it,
From east, west, north, and south. Be it concluded,
No barricado for a belly. Know't,
It will let in and out the enemy
With bag and baggage. Many thousand on's   205
Have the disease and feel't not. How now, boy?

Mamillius. I am like you, they say.

Leontes.   Why, that's some comfort.
What, Camillo there?

Camillo. Ay, my good lord.

Leontes. Go play, Mamillius. Thou'rt an honest man.   210

                              [*Exit Mamillius.*]

Camillo, this great sir will yet stay longer.

Camillo. You had much ado to make his anchor hold;
When you cast out, it still came home.

Leontes.   Didst note it?

Camillo. He would not stay at your petitions, made
His business more material.

Leontes.   Didst perceive it?   215
[*Aside*] They're here with me already, whispering, round-
  ing
'Sicilia is a so-forth.' 'Tis far gone,

200–201 *It is . . . predominant* unchastity, like a baneful planet, destroys
when in ascendant 205 *on's* of us 213 *still* always 216–17 *They're here . . .
so-forth* people are already mocking me, whispering I am a so-and-so
(perhaps Leontes, unable to say *cuckold*, puts two fingers to his head to
suggest horns)

When I shall gust it last. How came't, Camillo,
That he did stay?

Camillo.   At the good queen's entreaty.

220 *Leontes.* At the queen's be't. 'Good' should be pertinent;
But so it is, it is not. Was this taken
By any understanding pate but thine?
For thy conceit is soaking, will draw in
More than the common blocks. Not noted, is't,

225 But of the finer natures, by some severals
Of head-piece extraordinary? Lower messes
Perchance are to this business purblind? Say.

Camillo. Business, my lord? I think most understand
Bohemia stays here longer.

Leontes.   Ha?

Camillo.   Stays here longer.

230 *Leontes.* Ay, but why?

Camillo. To satisfy your highness and th' entreaties
Of our most gracious mistress.

Leontes.   Satisfy
The entreaties of your mistress? Satisfy;
Let that suffice. I have trusted thee, Camillo,

235 With all the nearest things to my heart, as well
My chamber-councils, wherein, priest-like, thou
Hast cleansed my bosom, I from thee departed
Thy penitent reformed. But we have been
Deceived in thy integrity, deceived
In that which seems so.

240 *Camillo.*   Be it forbid, my lord!

Leontes. To bide upon't, thou art not honest; or,

---

218 *gust* taste   221 *so* as   *taken* recognized   223 *conceit is soaking* understanding is absorbing   225 *severals* individuals   226 *Lower messes* inferior men (who at table occupy lower seats)   227 *purblind* wholly blind   241 *bide* dwell

If thou inclin'st that way, thou art a coward,
Which hoxes honesty behind, restraining
From course required; or else thou must be counted
A servant grafted in my serious trust   245
And therein negligent; or else a fool
That seest a game played home, the rich stake drawn,
And tak'st it all for jest.

Camillo.   My gracious lord,
I may be negligent, foolish, and fearful.
In every one of these no man is free,   250
But that his negligence, his folly, fear,
Among the infinite doings of the world,
Sometime puts forth. In your affairs, my lord,
If ever I were willful-negligent,
It was my folly; if industriously   255
I played the fool, it was my negligence,
Not weighing well the end; if ever fearful
To do a thing where I the issue doubted,
Whereof the execution did cry out
Against the non-performance, 'twas a fear   260
Which oft infects the wisest. These, my lord,
Are such allowed infirmities that honesty
Is never free of. But, beseech your grace,
Be plainer with me; let me know my trespass
By its own visage. If I then deny it,   265
'Tis none of mine.

Leontes.   Ha' not you seen, Camillo —
But that's past doubt, you have, or your eye-glass
Is thicker than a cuckold's horn — or heard —
For to a vision so apparent rumor

243 *hoxes* disables 245 *grafted . . . trust* insinuated into my confidence
253 *puts forth* reveals itself 255 *industriously* willfully 267 *eye-glass*
crystalline lens of the eye 268 *thicker* more opaque

37

270 Cannot be mute — or thought — for cogitation
Resides not in that man that does not think —
My wife is slippery? If thou wilt confess,
Or else be impudently negative,
To have nor eyes nor ears nor thought, then say
275 My wife's a hobby-horse, deserves a name
As rank as any flax-wench that puts to
Before her troth-plight. Say't and justify't.
Camillo. I would not be a stander-by to hear
My sovereign mistress clouded so, without
280 My present vengeance taken. 'Shrew my heart,
You never spoke what did become you less
Than this, which to reiterate were sin
As deep as that, though true.
Leontes.   Is whispering nothing?
Is leaning cheek to cheek? Is meeting noses?
285 Kissing with inside lip? stopping the career
Of laughter with a sigh? — a note infallible
Of breaking honesty! — horsing foot on foot?
Skulking in corners? wishing clocks more swift?
Hours, minutes? noon, midnight? and all eyes
290 Blind with the pin and web but theirs, theirs only,
That would unseen be wicked? Is this nothing?
Why, then the world and all that's in't is nothing,
The covering sky is nothing, Bohemia nothing,
My wife is nothing, nor nothing have these
       nothings,
If this be nothing.
295 *Camillo.*   Good my lord, be cured

---

280 *present* immediate *'Shrew* beshrew, curse 282–83 *which . . . true*
to repeat the charge against her would be a sin as great as her infidelity
were she guilty 285 *career* full gallop 287 *honesty* chastity 290 *pin and
web* cataract

Of this diseased opinion, and betimes,
For 'tis most dangerous.
Leontes.   Say it be, 'tis true.
Camillo. No, no, my lord.
Leontes.   It is. You lie, you lie.
I say thou liest, Camillo, and I hate thee,
Pronounce thee a gross lout, a mindless slave,   300
Or else a hovering temporizer, that
Canst with thine eyes at once see good and evil,
Inclining to them both. Were my wife's liver
Infected as her life, she would not live
The running of one glass.
Camillo.   Who does infect her?   305
Leontes. Why, he that wears her like her medal, hanging
About his neck — Bohemia, who, if I
Had servants true about me that bare eyes
To see alike mine honor as their profits,
Their own particular thrifts, they would do that   310
Which should undo more doing. Ay, and thou,
His cupbearer — whom I from meaner form
Have benched and reared to worship, who may'st see
Plainly as heaven sees earth and earth sees heaven,
How I am gallèd — might'st bespice a cup   315
To give mine enemy a lasting wink,
Which draught to me were cordial.
Camillo.   Sir, my lord,
I could do this, and that with no rash potion,
But with a ling'ring dram that should not work
Maliciously like poison. But I cannot   320
Believe this crack to be in my dread mistress,

296 *betimes* at once   301 *hovering* irresolute   305 *glass* hourglass   312
meaner form humbler position   313 *benched* placed in authority   *worship*
position of honor

So sovereignly being honorable.
I have loved thee —

Leontes.   Make that thy question, and go rot!
Dost think I am so muddy, so unsettled,
325 To appoint myself in this vexation, sully
The purity and whiteness of my sheets —
Which to preserve is sleep, which being spotted
Is goads, thorns, nettles, tails of wasps —
Give scandal to the blood o' th' prince my son,
330 Who I do think is mine and love as mine,
Without ripe moving to't? Would I do this?
Could man so blench?

Camillo.   I must believe you, sir.
I do, and will fetch off Bohemia for't;
Provided that, when he's removed, your highness
335 Will take again your queen as yours at first,
Even for your son's sake, and thereby forsealing
The injury of tongues in courts and kingdoms
Known and allied to yours.

Leontes.   Thou dost advise me
Even so as I mine own course have set down.
I'll give no blemish to her honor, none.

340 *Camillo.*   My lord,
Go then, and with a countenance as clear
As friendship wears at feasts, keep with Bohemia
And with your queen. I am his cupbearer.
If from me he have wholesome beverage,
Account me not your servant.

345 *Leontes.*   This is all.

---

323 (as Camillo would hardly be expected to use *thee* in addressing his
king, some editors assign the entire line to Leontes) 331 *Without ripe
moving* without good reason (the phrase goes with *appoint, sully, give
scandal*) 332 *blench* deceive himself 336 *forsealing* sealing tightly

Do't, and thou hast the one half of my heart;
Do't not, thou split'st thine own.
Camillo.   I'll do't, my lord.
Leontes. I will seem friendly, as thou hast advised me.
                                             [*Exit.*]

Camillo. O miserable lady! But for me,
  What case stand I in? I must be the poisoner   350
  Of good Polixenes; and my ground to do't
  Is the obedience to a master, one
  Who in rebellion with himself will have
  All that are his so too. To do this deed,
  Promotion follows. If I could find example   355
  Of thousands that had struck anointed kings
  And flourished after, I'ld not do't; but since
  Nor brass nor stone nor parchment bears not one,
  Let villainy itself forswear't. I must
  Forsake the court. To do't, or no, is certain   360
  To me a break-neck. Happy star reign now!
  Here comes Bohemia.

Enter Polixenes.

Polixenes.   This is strange. Methinks
  My favor here begins to warp. Not speak?
  Good day, Camillo.
Camillo.   Hail, most royal sir!
Polixenes. What is the news i' the court?
Camillo.   None rare, my lord.   365
Polixenes. The king hath on him such a countenance
  As he had lost some province and a region

354 *so too* i.e. in rebellion against (false to) themselves   360 *To do't* to
kill Polixenes   361 *Happy star* good fortune   363 *Not speak* (Polixenes
refers to Leontes, whom he encountered on his way in)   365 *rare* unusual

41

Loved as he loves himself. Even now I met him
With customary compliment, when he,
370   Wafting his eyes to th' contrary and falling
A lip of much contempt, speeds from me, and
So leaves me to consider what is breeding
That changeth thus his manners.

Camillo. I dare not know, my lord.

Polixenes. How dare not? do not? Do you know and dare
375   not
Be intelligent to me? 'Tis thereabouts,
For, to yourself, what you do know, you must,
And cannot say you dare not. Good Camillo,
Your changed complexions are to me a mirror
380   Which shows me mine changed too, for I must be
A party in this alteration, finding
Myself thus altered with't.

Camillo.   There is a sickness
Which puts some of us in distemper, but
I cannot name the disease, and it is caught
Of you that yet are well.

385 *Polixenes.*   How caught of me?
Make me not sighted like the basilisk.
I have looked on thousands who have sped the better
By my regard, but killed none so. Camillo,
As you are certainly a gentleman, thereto
390   Clerk-like experienced – which no less adorns
Our gentry than our parents' noble names,
In whose success we are gentle – I beseech you,
If you know aught which does behove my knowledge

368 *met* greeted   376 *intelligent* intelligible   '*Tis thereabouts* it is something
of the sort   386 *Make . . . basilisk* attribute not to me a sight like that of the
fabulous serpent whose look or breath was fatal   388 *regard* look   390
Clerk-like like a scholar   392 *In whose success* in succession from whom

Thereof to be informed, imprison't not
In ignorant concealment.

Camillo.   I may not answer.   395

Polixenes. A sickness caught of me, and yet I well?
I must be answered. Dost thou hear, Camillo?
I conjure thee by all the parts of man
Which honor does acknowledge, whereof the least
Is not this suit of mine, that thou declare   400
What incidency thou dost guess of harm
Is creeping toward me; how far off, how near;
Which way to be prevented, if to be;
If not, how best to bear it.

Camillo.   Sir, I will tell you,
Since I am charged in honor and by him   405
That I think honorable. Therefore mark my counsel,
Which must be even as swiftly followed as
I mean to utter it, or both yourself and me
Cry 'Lost,' and so good night!

Polixenes.   On, good Camillo.

Camillo. I am appointed him to murder you.   410

Polixenes. By whom, Camillo?

Camillo.   By the king.

Polixenes.   For what?

Camillo. He thinks, nay, with all confidence he swears,
As he had seen't or been an instrument
To vice you to't, that you have touched his queen
Forbiddenly.

Polixenes.   O, then my best blood turn   415
To an infected jelly and my name
Be yoked with his that did betray the Best!
Turn then my freshest reputation to

401 *incidency* happening 409 *good night* this is the end (as in modern slang,
an expression of finality) 414 *vice* force

A savor that may strike the dullest nostril
420 Where I arrive, and my approach be shunned,
Nay, hated too, worse than the great'st infection
That e'er was heard or read!

Camillo.   Swear his thought over
By each particular star in heaven and
By all their influences, you may as well
425 Forbid the sea for to obey the moon
As or by oath remove or counsel shake
The fabric of his folly, whose foundation
Is piled upon his faith and will continue
The standing of his body.

Polixenes.   How should this grow?
430 Camillo. I know not. But I am sure 'tis safer to
Avoid what's grown than question how 'tis born.
If therefore you dare trust my honesty,
That lies enclosèd in this trunk which you
Shall bear along impawned, away to-night!
435 Your followers I will whisper to the business,
And will by twos and threes at several posterns
Clear them o' th' city. For myself, I'll put
My fortunes to your service, which are here
By this discovery lost. Be not uncertain,
440 For, by the honor of my parents, I
Have uttered truth, which if you seek to prove,
I dare not stand by; nor shall you be safer
Than one condemnèd by the king's own mouth,
Thereon his execution sworn.

Polixenes.   I do believe thee;
445 I saw his heart in's face. Give me thy hand.

---

426 *or . . . or* either . . . or   427 *fabric* creation   433 *trunk* body   434 *impawned* as a pledge   435 *whisper to* secretly tell of   436 *posterns* back doors

Be pilot to me and thy places shall
Still neighbor mine. My ships are ready and
My people did expect my hence departure
Two days ago. This jealousy
Is for a precious creature. As she's rare,   450
Must it be great; and as his person's mighty,
Must it be violent; and as he does conceive
He is dishonored by a man which ever
Professed to him, why, his revenges must
In that be made more bitter. Fear o'ershades me.   455
Good expedition be my friend, and comfort
The gracious queen, part of his theme but nothing
Of his ill-ta'en suspicion! Come, Camillo.
I will respect thee as a father if
Thou bear'st my life off hence. Let us avoid.   460
Camillo. It is in mine authority to command
The keys of all the posterns. Please your highness
To take the urgent hour. Come, sir, away.   *Exeunt.*

Enter Hermione, Mamillius, Ladies.   II, i

Hermione. Take the boy to you. He so troubles me,
'Tis past enduring.
Lady.   Come, my gracious lord,
Shall I be your playfellow?
Mamillius.   No, I'll none of you.

446–47 *thy places . . . mine* i.e. you may always have an appointment in my
household   454 *Professed* professed love   455 *o'ershades* covers   456 *expedition* prompt action   460 *avoid* depart   II, i, 1 *Take . . . to you* take
charge of the boy

Lady. Why, my sweet lord?

5 *Mamillius.* You'll kiss me hard and speak to me as if
I were a baby still. I love you better.

Second Lady. And why so, my lord?

Mamillius.   Not for because
Your brows are blacker. Yet black brows, they say,
Become some women best, so that there be not

10 Too much hair there, but in a semicircle,
Or a half-moon made with a pen.

Second Lady.   Who taught' this?

Mamillius. I learned it out of women's faces. Pray now,
What color are your eyebrows?

Lady.   Blue, my lord.

Mamillius. Nay, that's a mock. I have seen a lady's nose
That has been blue, but not her eyebrows.

15 *Lady.*   Hark ye.
The queen your mother rounds apace. We shall
Present our services to a fine new prince
One of these days, and then you'ld wanton with us,
If we would have you.

Second Lady.   She is spread of late

20 Into a goodly bulk. Good time encounter her!

Hermione. What wisdom stirs amongst you? Come, sir,
now
I am for you again. Pray you sit by us
And tell's a tale.

Mamillius.   Merry or sad shall't be?

Hermione. As merry as you will.

25 *Mamillius.* A sad tale's best for winter. I have one
Of sprites and goblins.

Hermione.   Let's have that, good sir.

---

11 *taught'* taught thee 18 *wanton* play 20 *Good time encounter* good fortune
attend 21 *wisdom stirs* wise matter is discussed

Come on, sit down. Come on, and do your best
To fright me with your sprites; you're powerful at it.
Mamillius. There was a man —
Hermione.   Nay, come sit down; then on.
Mamillius. Dwelt by a churchyard. I will tell it softly;   30
Yond crickets shall not hear it.
Hermione.   Come on, then,
And give't me in mine ear.

[*Enter*] *Leontes, Antigonus, Lords, [and others*].

Leontes. Was he met there? his train? Camillo with him?
Lord. Behind the tuft of pines I met them. Never
Saw I men scour so on their way. I eyed them   35
Even to their ships.
Leontes.   How blest am I
In my just censure, in my true opinion!
Alack, for lesser knowledge! how accursed
In being so blest! There may be in the cup
A spider steeped, and one may drink, depart,   40
And yet partake no venom, for his knowledge
Is not infected; but if one present
Th' abhorred ingredient to his eye, make known
How he hath drunk, he cracks his gorge, his sides,
With violent hefts. I have drunk, and seen the spider.   45
Camillo was his help in this, his pander.
There is a plot against my life, my crown.
All's true that is mistrusted. That false villain
Whom I employed was pre-employed by him.
He has discovered my design, and I   50

31 *crickets* i.e. the 'ladies in waiting with their tittering and chirping laughter' (Furness) 35 *scour* hasten 38 *Alack . . . knowledge* O, that my knowledge were less 45 *hefts* heavings 50 *discovered* revealed

47

Remain a pinched thing — yea, a very trick
For them to play at will. How came the posterns
So easily open?

Lord.   By his great authority,
Which often hath no less prevailed than so
On your command.

55 *Leontes.*   I know't too well.
Give me the boy. I am glad you did not nurse him.
Though he does bear some signs of me, yet you
Have too much blood in him.

Hermione.   What is this? sport?

Leontes. Bear the boy hence. He shall not come about her.
60 Away with him! and let her sport herself
With that she's big with, for 'tis Polixenes
Has made thee swell thus.

Hermione.   But I'd say he had not,
And I'll be sworn you would believe my saying,
Howe'er you lean to the nayward.

Leontes.   You, my lords,
65 Look on her, mark her well. Be but about
To say 'She is a goodly lady,' and
The justice of your hearts will thereto add
"Tis pity she's not honest, honorable.'
Praise her but for this her without-door form —
70 Which on my faith deserves high speech — and straight
The shrug, the hum or ha, these petty brands
That calumny doth use — O, I am out,
That mercy does, for calumny will sear
Virtue itself — these shrugs, these hums and ha's,
75 When you have said she's goodly, come between

51 *a pinched thing* 'a wretch upon the rack' (Wilson), 'a puppet' (Heath)
trick toy   58 *sport* jesting   64 *nayward* negative   69 *without-door form*
outward appearance   72 *out* mistaken   75 *come between* interfere

Ere you can say she's honest. But be't known,
From him that has most cause to grieve it should be,
She's an adult'ress.

Hermione.   Should a villain say so,
The most replenished villain in the world,
He were as much more villain. You, my lord,   80
Do but mistake.

Leontes.   You have mistook, my lady,
Polixenes for Leontes. O thou thing!
Which I'll not call a creature of thy place,
Lest barbarism, making me the precedent,
Should a like language use to all degrees   85
And mannerly distinguishment leave out
Betwixt the prince and beggar. I have said
She's an adult'ress; I have said with whom.
More, she's a traitor and Camillo is
A federary with her, and one that knows   90
What she should shame to know herself
But with her most vile principal, that she's
A bed-swerver, even as bad as those
That vulgars give bold'st titles — ay, and privy
To this their late escape.

Hermione.   No, by my life,   95
Privy to none of this. How will this grieve you,
When you shall come to clearer knowledge, that
You thus have published me! Gentle my lord,
You scarce can right me throughly then to say
You did mistake.

Leontes.   No. If I mistake   100
In those foundations which I build upon,

79 *replenished* full   83 *place* rank   90 *federary* confederate   93 *bed-swerver* adulteress   94 *vulgars . . . titles* common people call rudest names
99 *throughly* thoroughly

The center is not big enough to bear
A schoolboy's top. Away with her to prison!
He who shall speak for her is afar off guilty
But that he speaks.
105 *Hermione.*   There's some ill planet reigns.
I must be patient till the heavens look
With an aspect more favorable. Good my lords,
I am not prone to weeping, as our sex
Commonly are; the want of which vain dew
110 Perchance shall dry your pities. But I have
That honorable grief lodged here which burns
Worse than tears drown. Beseech you all, my lords,
With thoughts so qualified as your charities
Shall best instruct you, measure me; and so
The king's will be performed.
115 *Leontes.*   Shall I be heard?
Hermione. Who is't that goes with me? Beseech your high-
    ness,
My women may be with me, for you see
My plight requires it. Do not weep, good fools;
There is no cause. When you shall know your mistress
120 Has deserved prison, then abound in tears
As I come out. This action I now go on
Is for my better grace. Adieu, my lord.
I never wished to see you sorry; now
I trust I shall. My women, come; you have leave.
125 *Leontes.* Go, do our bidding. Hence!
                [Exit Queen, guarded, with Ladies.]
Lord. Beseech your highness, call the queen again.
Antigonus. Be certain what you do, sir, lest your justice

---

102 *center* earth   104–5 *He . . . speaks* he is indirectly guilty who merely
speaks in her behalf   113 *qualified* modified   114 *measure* judge   118 *fools*
(a term of endearment)

Prove violence, in the which three great ones suffer,
Yourself, your queen, your son.

Lord. For her, my lord,
  I dare my life lay down and will do't, sir, 130
  Please you t' accept it, that the queen is spotless
  I' th' eyes of heaven and to you — I mean,
  In this which you accuse her.

Antigonus. If it prove
  She's otherwise, I'll keep my stables where
  I lodge my wife. I'll go in couples with her, 135
  Than when I feel and see her no farther trust her;
  For every inch of woman in the world,
  Ay, every dram of woman's flesh is false,
  If she be.

Leontes. Hold your peaces.

Lord. Good my lord —

Antigonus. It is for you we speak, not for ourselves. 140
  You are abused and by some putter-on
  That will be damned for't. Would I knew the villain,
  I would land-damn him. Be she honor-flawed,
  I have three daughters — the eldest is eleven,
  The second and the third, nine and some five — 145
  If this prove true, they'll pay for't. By mine honor,
  I'll geld 'em all; fourteen they shall not see
  To bring false generations. They are co-heirs,
  And I had rather glib myself than they
  Should not produce fair issue.

Leontes. Cease; no more. 150
  You smell this business with a sense as cold

---

128 *violence* outrage   134–35 *I'll . . . her* (perhaps in part the meaning of
this puzzling passage is: 'I'll guard the stables where my wife lives and
never leave her alone'—*stables* intended to suggest a beast to be ridden)
143 *land-damn* (the *damn* reveals the meaning of this 'mysterious com-
pound')   149 *glib* geld

As is a dead man's nose; but I do see't and feel't,
As you feel doing thus [*pinches Antigonus*], and see withal
The instruments that feel.

Antigonus.   If it be so,
155   We need no grave to bury honesty;
There's not a grain of it the face to sweeten
Of the whole dungy earth.

Leontes.   What? Lack I credit?

Lord. I had rather you did lack than I, my lord,
Upon this ground; and more it would content me
160   To have her honor true than your suspicion,
Be blamed for't how you might.

Leontes.   Why, what need we
Commune with you of this, but rather follow
Our forceful instigation? Our prerogative
Calls not your counsels, but our natural goodness
165   Imparts this, which if you — or stupefied
Or seeming so in skill — cannot or will not
Relish a truth like us, inform yourselves
We need no more of your advice. The matter,
The loss, the gain, the ordering on't, is all
Properly ours.

170 *Antigonus.*   And I wish, my liege,
You had only in your silent judgment tried it,
Without more overture.

Leontes.   How could that be?
Either thou art most ignorant by age
Or thou wert born a fool. Camillo's flight,
175   Added to their familiarity —
Which was as gross as ever touched conjecture,

154 *instruments that feel* i.e. Leontes' fingers   159 *ground* matter   163 *insti-gation* incentive   164 *Calls* calls for   165 *Imparts* bestows   166 *skill* discern-ment   172 *overture* public revelation

That lacked sight only, nought for approbation
But only seeing, all other circumstances
Made up to th' deed — doth push on this proceeding.
Yet, for a greater confirmation —   180
For in an act of this importance 'twere
Most piteous to be wild — I have dispatched in post
To sacred Delphos, to Apollo's temple,
Cleomenes and Dion, whom you know
Of stuffed sufficiency. Now from the oracle   185
They will bring all, whose spiritual counsel had,
Shall stop or spur me. Have I done well?

Lord. Well done, my lord.

Leontes. Though I am satisfied and need no more
Than what I know, yet shall the oracle   190
Give rest to th' minds of others, such as he
Whose ignorant credulity will not
Come up to th' truth. So have we thought it good
From our free person she should be confined,
Lest that the treachery of the two fled hence   195
Be left her to perform. Come, follow us.
We are to speak in public, for this business
Will raise us all.

Antigonus.   [*aside*] To laughter, as I take it,
If the good truth were known.   *Exeunt.*

182 *wild* rash   *post* haste   185 *stuffed sufficiency* full competence   193
Come up to face   194 *free* easily accessible   198 *raise* rouse to action

     Enter Paulina, a Gentleman, [and Attendants].

Paulina. The keeper of the prison, call to him;
   Let him have knowledge who I am.   *[Exit Gentleman.]*
                   Good lady,
   No court in Europe is too good for thee.
   What dost thou then in prison?

         [Enter Gentleman with the] Gaoler.

                  Now, good sir,
   You know me, do you not?
5 *Gaoler.*   For a worthy lady
   And one whom much I honor.
   Paulina.   Pray you then,
   Conduct me to the queen.
   Gaoler.   I may not, madam.
   To the contrary I have express commandment.
   Paulina. Here's ado,
10   To lock up honesty and honor from
   Th' access of gentle visitors. Is't lawful, pray you,
   To see her women? any of them? Emilia?
   Gaoler. So please you, madam,
   To put apart these your attendants, I
   Shall bring Emilia forth.
15 *Paulina.*   I pray now, call her.
   Withdraw yourselves.
             [Exeunt Gentleman and Attendants.]
   Gaoler.   And, madam,
   I must be present at your conference.
   Paulina. Well, be't so, prithee.   *[Exit Gaoler.]*
   Here's such ado to make no stain a stain
   As passes coloring.

   II, ii, 20 *passes* surpasses

[Enter Gaoler with] Emilia.

                        Dear gentlewoman,   20
How fares our gracious lady?

Emilia. As well as one so great and so forlorn
  May hold together. On her frights and griefs,
  Which never tender lady hath borne greater,
  She is something before her time delivered.   25

Paulina. A boy?

Emilia.   A daughter, and a goodly babe,
  Lusty and like to live. The queen receives
  Much comfort in't, says, 'My poor prisoner,
  I am innocent as you.'

Paulina.   I dare be sworn.
  These dangerous unsafe lunes i' th' king, beshrew them!   30
  He must be told on't, and he shall. The office
  Becomes a woman best; I'll take't upon me.
  If I prove honey-mouthed, let my tongue blister
  And never to my red-looked anger be
  The trumpet any more. Pray you, Emilia,   35
  Commend my best obedience to the queen.
  If she dares trust me with her little babe,
  I'll show't the king and undertake to be
  Her advocate to th' loud'st. We do not know
  How he may soften at the sight o' th' child.   40
  The silence often of pure innocence
  Persuades when speaking fails.

Emilia.   Most worthy madam,
  Your honor and your goodness is so evident
  That your free undertaking cannot miss
  A thriving issue. There is no lady living   45

25 *something* somewhat   30 *lunes* fits of lunacy   34 *red-looked* red-faced
44 *free* voluntary

So meet for this great errand. Please your ladyship
To visit the next room, I'll presently
Acquaint the queen of your most noble offer,
Who but to-day hammered of this design,
50   But durst not tempt a minister of honor
Lest she should be denied.

Paulina.   Tell her, Emilia,
I'll use that tongue I have. If wit flow from't
As boldness from my bosom, let 't not be doubted
I shall do good.

Emilia.   Now be you blest for it!
55   I'll to the queen. Please you, come something nearer.

Gaoler. Madam, if't please the queen to send the babe,
I know not what I shall incur to pass it,
Having no warrant.

Paulina.   You need not fear it, sir.
This child was prisoner to the womb and is
60   By law and process of great nature thence
Freed and enfranchised, not a party to
The anger of the king nor guilty of,
If any be, the trespass of the queen.

Gaoler. I do believe it.

65 *Paulina.* Do not you fear. Upon mine honor, I
Will stand betwixt you and danger.   *Exeunt.*

II, iii   *Enter Leontes, Servants, Antigonus, and Lords.*

Leontes. Nor night nor day no rest. It is but weakness
To bear the matter thus — mere weakness. If
The cause were not in being — part o' th' cause,

47 *presently* at once 49 *hammered of* formulated 50 *tempt* try to win over

She, the adult'ress; for the harlot king
Is quite beyond mine arm, out of the blank   5
And level of my brain, plot-proof. But she
I can hook to me. Say that she were gone,
Given to the fire, a moiety of my rest
Might come to me again. Who's there?

Servant.   My lord.

Leontes. How does the boy?

Servant.   He took good rest to-night.   10
'Tis hoped his sickness is discharged.

Leontes. To see his nobleness!
Conceiving the dishonor of his mother,
He straight declined, drooped, took it deeply,
Fastened and fixed the shame on't in himself,   15
Threw off his spirit, his appetite, his sleep,
And downright languished. Leave me solely. Go
See how he fares. *[Exit Servant.]* Fie, fie! no thought of
    him!
The very thought of my revenges that way
Recoil upon me — in himself too mighty,   20
And in his parties, his alliance. Let him be
Until a time may serve. For present vengeance,
Take it on her. Camillo and Polixenes
Laugh at me, make their pastime at my sorrow.
They should not laugh if I could reach them, nor   25
Shall she within my power.

Enter Paulina [with a Babe].

Lord.   You must not enter.

Paulina. Nay, rather, good my lords, be second to me.

II, iii, 4 *harlot* (originally of either sex) 5–6 *blank And level* target and
aim 8 *moiety* part 15 *on't* of it 17 *solely* alone 18 *him* i.e. Polixenes
27 *be second to* assist

Fear you his tyrannous passion more, alas,
Than the queen's life? a gracious innocent soul,
More free than he is jealous.

30 *Antigonus.*   That's enough.

Servant. Madam, he hath not slept to-night, commanded
None should come at him.

Paulina.   Not so hot, good sir.
I come to bring him sleep. 'Tis such as you,
That creep like shadows by him and do sigh

35 At each his needless heavings, such as you
Nourish the cause of his awaking. I
Do come with words as medicinal as true,
Honest as either, to purge him of that humor
That presses him from sleep.

Leontes.   What noise there, ho?

40 *Paulina.* No noise, my lord, but needful conference
About some gossips for your highness.

Leontes.   How?
Away with that audacious lady! Antigonus,
I charged thee that she should not come about me.
I knew she would.

Antigonus.   I told her so, my lord,

45 On your displeasure's peril and on mine,
She should not visit you.

Leontes.   What, canst not rule her?

Paulina. From all dishonesty he can. In this,
Unless he take the course that you have done,
Commit me for committing honor, trust it,
He shall not rule me.

50 *Antigonus.*   La you now, you hear!

30 *free* innocent   38 *humor* that of the four humors which, by having become predominant, prevented sleep   41 *gossips* godparents for the child
49 *Commit* imprison

58

When she will take the rein I let her run,
But she'll not stumble.
Paulina.   Good my liege, I come —
And I beseech you hear me, who profess
Myself your loyal servant, your physician,
Your most obedient counsellor, yet that dare   55
Less appear so in comforting your evils
Than such as most seem yours — I say I come
From your good queen.
Leontes.   Good queen?
Paulina.   Good queen, my lord,
Good queen. I say good queen,
And would by combat make her good, so were I   60
A man, the worst about you.
Leontes.   Force her hence.
Paulina. Let him that makes but trifles of his eyes
First hand me. On mine own accord I'll off,
But first I'll do my errand. The good queen,
For she is good, hath brought you forth a daughter —   65
Here 'tis — commends it to your blessing.
                         [Lays down the child.]
Leontes.   Out!
A mankind witch! Hence with her, out o' door!
A most intelligencing bawd.
Paulina.   Not so.
I am as ignorant in that as you
In so entitling me — and no less honest   70
Than you are mad, which is enough, I'll warrant,
As this world goes, to pass for honest.
Leontes.   Traitors!
Will you not push her out? Give her the bastard.

56 *comforting* condoning 67 *mankind* masculine 68 *intelligencing* spying

Thou dotard, thou art woman-tired, unroosted
75   By thy dame Partlet here. Take up the bastard.
     Take't up, I say. Give't to thy crone.

Paulina.   For ever
     Unvenerable be thy hands, if thou
     Tak'st up the princess by that forcèd baseness
     Which he has put upon't!

Leontes.   He dreads his wife.

80 *Paulina.* So I would you did. Then 'twere past all doubt
     You'ld call your children yours.

Leontes.   A nest of traitors!

Antigonus. I am none, by this good light.

Paulina.   Nor I, nor any
     But one that's here, and that's himself; for he
     The sacred honor of himself, his queen's,
85   His hopeful son's, his babe's, betrays to slander,
     Whose sting is sharper than the sword's; and will not —
     For, as the case now stands, it is a curse
     He cannot be compelled to't — once remove
     The root of his opinion, which is rotten
     As ever oak or stone was sound.

90 *Leontes.*   A callet
     Of boundless tongue, who late hath beat her husband
     And now baits me! This brat is none of mine;
     It is the issue of Polixenes.
     Hence with it, and together with the dam
     Commit them to the fire!

95 *Paulina.*   It is yours,
     And, might we lay th' old proverb to your charge,

---

74 *dotard* imbecile *woman-tired, unroosted* henpecked, driven from the
roost 75 *Partlet* Pertelote (the hen in Chaucer's Nun's Priest's Tale, whose
dominance of her husband almost brought his ruin) 78 *forcèd baseness*
false designation as bastard 90 *callet* scold

So like you 'tis the worse. Behold, my lords.
Although the print be little, the whole matter
And copy of the father – eye, nose, lip,
The trick of's frown, his forehead, nay, the valley,   100
The pretty dimples of his chin and cheek, his smiles,
The very mould and frame of hand, nail, finger.
And thou, good goddess Nature, which hast made it
So like to him that got it, if thou hast
The ordering of the mind too, 'mongst all colors   105
No yellow in't, lest she suspect, as he does,
Her children not her husband's!

Leontes.   A gross hag!
And, lozel, thou art worthy to be hanged
That wilt not stay her tongue.

Antigonus.   Hang all the husbands
That cannot do that feat, you'll leave yourself   110
Hardly one subject.

Leontes.   Once more, take her hence!

Paulina. A most unworthy and unnatural lord
Can do no more.

Leontes.   I'll ha' thee burnt.

Paulina.   I care not.
It is an heretic that makes the fire,
Not she which burns in't. I'll not call you tyrant;   115
But this most cruel usage of your queen,
Not able to produce more accusation
Than your own weak-hinged fancy, something savors
Of tyranny and will ignoble make you,
Yea, scandalous to the world.

---

100 *valley* cleft in chin (?) or, crease in forehead (?)   104 *got* begot   106
yellow (the color of jealousy)   107 (in her righteous rage Paulina fails to
realize that jealousy would not in a wife engender doubts as to the father of
her children)   108 *lozel* worthless person

61

120 *Leontes.*   On your allegiance,
     Out of the chamber with her! Were I a tyrant,
     Where were her life? She durst not call me so
     If she did know me one. Away with her!
     Paulina. I pray you do not push me; I'll be gone.
125 Look to your babe, my lord; 'tis yours. Jove send her
     A better guiding spirit. What needs these hands?
     You that are thus so tender o'er his follies
     Will never do him good, not one of you.
     So, so. Farewell; we are gone.   *Exit.*
130 *Leontes.* Thou, traitor, hast set on thy wife to this.
     My child? away with't! Even thou, that hast
     A heart so tender o'er it, take it hence
     And see it instantly consumed with fire –
     Even thou and none but thou. Take it up straight.
135 Within this hour bring me word 'tis done,
     And by good testimony, or I'll seize thy life,
     With what thou else call'st thine. If thou refuse
     And wilt encounter with my wrath, say so.
     The bastard brains with these my proper hands
140 Shall I dash out. Go, take it to the fire,
     For thou set'st on thy wife.
     Antigonus.   I did not, sir.
     These lords, my noble fellows, if they please,
     Can clear me in't.
     Lords.   We can. My royal liege,
     He is not guilty of her coming hither.
145 *Leontes.* You're liars all.
     Lord. Beseech your highness, give us better credit.
     We have always truly served you, and beseech you
     So to esteem of us; and on our knees we beg,

126 *these hands* i.e. those which push her   130 *Thou* i.e. Antigonus   139
proper own   147 *beseech you* (the folio, omitting *you*, prints *beseech'*)

As recompense of our dear services
Past and to come, that you do change this purpose,   150
Which being so horrible, so bloody, must
Lead on to some foul issue. We all kneel.

Leontes. I am a feather for each wind that blows.
Shall I live on to see this bastard kneel
And call me father? Better burn it now   155
Than curse it then. But be it; let it live.
It shall not neither. You, sir, come you hither,
You that have been so tenderly officious
With Lady Margery, your midwife there,
To save this bastard's life — for 'tis a bastard,   160
So sure as this beard's grey. What will you adventure
To save this brat's life?

Antigonus.   Anything, my lord,
That my ability may undergo
And nobleness impose. At least thus much.
I'll pawn the little blood which I have·left   165
To save the innocent. Anything possible.

Leontes. It shall be possible. Swear by this sword
Thou wilt perform my bidding.

Antigonus.   I will, my lord.

Leontes. Mark and perform it, seest thou; for the fail
Of any point in't shall not only be   170
Death to thyself but to thy lewd-tongued wife,
Whom for this time we pardon. We enjoin thee,
As thou art liege-man to us, that thou carry
This female bastard hence, and that thou bear it
To some remote and desert place quite out   175
Of our dominions, and that there thou leave it,

---

156 *be it* so be it 159 *Margery* hen (?) (Partridge records a cant term from
c. 1570, *Margery-prater* hen; cf. *Partlet*, line 75) 163 *undergo* perform.
165 *pawn* risk 169 *fail* failure

Without more mercy, to it own protection
And favor of the climate. As by strange fortune
It came to us, I do in justice charge thee,
180   On thy soul's peril and thy body's torture,
That thou commend it strangely to some place
Where chance may nurse or end it. Take it up.

Antigonus. I swear to do this, though a present death
Had been more merciful. Come on, poor babe.
185   Some powerful spirit instruct the kites and ravens
To be thy nurses. Wolves and bears, they say,
Casting their savageness aside, have done
Like offices of pity. Sir, be prosperous
In more than this deed does require. And blessing
190   Against this cruelty fight on thy side,
Poor thing, condemned to loss.   *Exit [with the Babe].*

Leontes.   No, I'll not rear
Another's issue.

Enter a Servant.

Servant.   Please your highness, posts
From those you sent to th' oracle are come
An hour since. Cleomenes and Dion,
195   Being well arrived from Delphos, are both landed,
Hasting to th' court.

Lord.   So please you, sir, their speed
Hath been beyond account.

Leontes.   Twenty-three days
They have been absent. 'Tis good speed, foretells
The great Apollo suddenly will have
200   The truth of this appear. Prepare you, lords;

177 *it* its (an earlier form of the possessive) 181 *commend . . . place* commit
it to some foreign place 189 *require* deserve 197 *account* record 199
suddenly at once

64

Summon a session, that we may arraign
Our most disloyal lady, for, as she hath
Been publicly accused, so shall she have
A just and open trial. While she lives
My heart will be a burthen to me. Leave me,   205
And think upon my bidding.   *Exeunt.*

Enter Cleomenes and Dion.   III, i

Cleomenes. The climate's delicate, the air most sweet,
  Fertile the isle, the temple much surpassing
  The common praise it bears.
Dion.   I shall report,
  For most it caught me, the celestial habits —
  Methinks I so should term them — and the reverence   5
  Of the grave wearers. O, the sacrifice,
  How ceremonious, solemn, and unearthly
  It was i' th' off'ring!
Cleomenes.   But of all, the burst
  And the ear-deaf'ning voice o' th' oracle,
  Kin to Jove's thunder, so surprised my sense   10
  That I was nothing.
Dion.   If th' event o' th' journey
  Prove as successful to the queen — O be't so! —
  As it hath been to us rare, pleasant, speedy,
  The time is worth the use on't.
Cleomenes.   Great Apollo
  Turn all to th' best! These proclamations,   15
  So forcing faults upon Hermione,
  I little like.

III, i, 2 *isle* (in making Delphi an island, as in providing Bohemia with a
seacoast, Shakespeare is following Greene)

65

Dion.   The violent carriage of it
          Will clear or end the business. When the oracle,
          Thus by Apollo's great divine sealed up,
20   Shall the contents discover, something rare
          Even then will rush to knowledge. Go. Fresh horses!
          And gracious be the issue!   *Exeunt.*

III, ii   *Enter Leontes, Lords, Officers.*

Leontes. This sessions, to our great grief we pronounce,
          Even pushes 'gainst our heart – the party tried
          The daughter of a king, our wife, and one
          Of us too much beloved. Let us be cleared
5   Of being tyrannous, since we so openly
          Proceed in justice, which shall have due course,
          Even to the guilt or the purgation.
          Produce the prisoner.
Officer. It is his highness' pleasure that the queen
10   Appear in person here in court. Silence!

          [Enter] Hermione, as to her trial, [Paulina, and] Ladies.

Leontes. Read the indictment.
Officer. *[reads]* Hermione, queen to the worthy Leontes,
          king of Sicilia, thou art here accused and arraigned of
          high treason, in committing adultery with Polixenes,
15   king of Bohemia, and conspiring with Camillo to take
          away the life of our sovereign lord the king, thy royal
          husband; the pretense whereof being by circumstances
          partly laid open, thou, Hermione, contrary to the faith

          III, ii, 4 *Of* by 7 *purgation* clearing 10 (the folio prints *Silence* as a stage
          direction) 17 *pretense* purpose

and allegiance of a true subject, didst counsel and aid
them, for their better safety, to fly away by night.   20

Hermione. Since what I am to say must be but that
Which contradicts my accusation, and
The testimony on my part no other
But what comes from myself, it shall scarce boot me
To say, 'Not guilty.' Mine integrity,   25
Being counted falsehood, shall, as I express it,
Be so received. But thus: if powers divine
Behold our human actions, as they do,
I doubt not then but innocence shall make
False accusation blush and tyranny   30
Tremble at patience. You, my lord, best know,
Who least will seem to do so, my past life
Hath been as continent, as chaste, as true,
As I am now unhappy; which is more
Than history can pattern, though devised   35
And played to take spectators. For behold me –
A fellow of the royal bed, which owe
A moiety of the throne, a great king's daughter,
The mother to a hopeful prince – here standing
To prate and talk for life and honor 'fore   40
Who please to come and hear. For life, I prize it
As I weigh grief, which I would spare. For honor,
'Tis a derivative from me to mine,
And only that I stand for. I appeal
To your own conscience, sir, before Polixenes   45
Came to your court, how I was in your grace,
How merited to be so; since he came,
With what encounter so uncurrent I

24 *boot* profit   35 *pattern* match   37 *owe* own   38 *moiety* share   43 *a
derivative . . . mine* something to be inherited by my children from me
48 *uncurrent* unlawful

Have strained t' appear thus; if one jot beyond
50 The bound of honor, or in act or will
That way inclining, hardened be the hearts
Of all that hear me, and my near'st of kin
Cry fie upon my grave!

Leontes.   I ne'er heard yet
That any of these bolder vices wanted
55 Less impudence to gainsay what they did
Than to perform it first.

Hermione.   That's true enough,
Though 'tis a saying, sir, not due to me.

Leontes. You will not own it.

Hermione.   More than mistress of
Which comes to me in name of fault, I must not
60 At all acknowledge. For Polixenes,
With whom I am accused, I do confess
I loved him as in honor he required —
With such a kind of love as might become
A lady like me, with a love even such,
65 So and no other, as yourself commanded —
Which not to have done I think had been in me
Both disobedience and ingratitude
To you and toward your friend, whose love had spoke,
Even since it could speak, from an infant, freely
70 That it was yours. Now, for conspiracy,
I know not how it tastes, though it be dished
For me to try how. All I know of it
Is that Camillo was an honest man;
And why he left your court, the gods themselves,
75 Wotting no more than I, are ignorant.

---

57 *due to me* applicable to my behavior   58–59 *More . . . fault* more faults
than I have   62 *required* deserved   75 *Wotting* if they know

Leontes. You knew of his departure, as you know
  What you have underta'en to do in's absence.

Hermione. Sir,
  You speak a language that I understand not.
  My life stands in the level of your dreams,   80
  Which I'll lay down.

Leontes.   Your actions are my dreams.
  You had a bastard by Polixenes,
  And I but dreamed it. As you were past all shame —
  Those of your fact are so — so past all truth,
  Which to deny concerns more than avails; for as   .85
  Thy brat hath been cast out, like to itself,
  No father owning it — which is, indeed,
  More criminal in thee than it — so thou
  Shalt feel our justice, in whose easiest passage
  Look for no less than death.

Hermione.   Sir, spare your threats.   90
  The bug which you would fright me with I seek.
  To me can life be no commodity.
  The crown and comfort of my life, your favor,
  I do give lost, for I do feel it gone,
  But know not how it went. My second joy   95
  And first-fruits of my body, from his presence
  I am barred, like one infectious. My third comfort,
  Starred most unluckily, is from my breast,
  The innocent milk in it most innocent mouth,
  Haled out to murder. Myself on every post   100
  Proclaimed a strumpet: with immodest hatred
  The child-bed privilege denied, which 'longs
  To women of all fashion. Lastly, hurried
  Here to this place, i' th' open air, before

80 *in* on 84 *fact* deed 85 *concerns* implicates 91 *bug* bugbear 92 *commodity* comfort 98 *Starred* fated 101 *immodest* immoderate

105   I have got strength of limit. Now, my liege,
Tell me what blessings I have here alive,
That I should fear to die? Therefore proceed.
But yet hear this — mistake me not, no life
(I prize it not a straw) but for mine honor,
110   Which I would free. If I shall be condemned
Upon surmises, all proofs sleeping else
But what your jealousies awake, I tell you
'Tis rigor and not law. Your honors all,
I do refer me to the oracle.
Apollo be my judge!

115 *Lord.*   This your request
Is altogether just. Therefore bring forth,
And in Apollo's name, his oracle.

                         [Exeunt certain Officers.]

Hermione. The emperor of Russia was my father.
O that he were alive, and here beholding
120   His daughter's trial; that he did but see
The flatness of my misery — yet with eyes
Of pity, not revenge.

      [Enter Officers with] Cleomenes, [and] Dion.

Officer. You here shall swear upon this sword of justice,
That you, Cleomenes and Dion, have
125   Been both at Delphos, and from thence have brought
This sealed-up oracle, by the hand delivered
Of great Apollo's priest, and that since then
You have not dared to break the holy seal
Nor read the secrets in't.

Cleomenes, Dion.   All this we swear.

130 *Leontes.* Break up the seals and read.

105 *of limit* limited 108–9 *no life . . . honor* I speak not to ask life but for my honor

70

Officer. [reads] Hermione is chaste, Polixenes blameless,
  Camillo a true subject, Leontes a jealous tyrant, his in-
  nocent babe truly begotten; and the king shall live with-
  out an heir if that which is lost be not found.
Lords. Now blessèd be the great Apollo!
Hermione.   Praised!   135
Leontes. Hast thou read truth?
Officer.   Ay, my lord, even so
  As it is here set down.
Leontes. There is no truth at all i' th' oracle.
  The sessions shall proceed. This is mere falsehood.

[Enter Servant.]

Servant. My lord the king, the king!
Leontes.   What is the business?   140
Servant. O sir, I shall be hated to report it.
  The prince your son, with mere conceit and fear
  Of the queen's speed, is gone.
Leontes.   How? gone?
Servant.   Is dead.
Leontes. Apollo's angry, and the heavens themselves
  Do strike at my injustice. *[Hermione swoons.]* How now
    there?   145
Paulina. This news is mortal to the queen. Look down
  And see what death is doing.
Leontes.   Take her hence.
  Her heart is but o'ercharged; she will recover.
  I have too much believed mine own suspicion.
  Beseech you, tenderly apply to her   150
  Some remedies for life.
            [Exeunt Paulina and Ladies with Hermione.]

139 *sessions* trial 142 *conceit* imagination *fear* anxiety 143 *speed* success
146 *mortal* fatal 148 *o'ercharged* too full (of grief)

                            Apollo, pardon
        My great profaneness 'gainst thine oracle!
        I'll reconcile me to Polixenes,
        New woo my queen, recall the good Camillo,
155   Whom I proclaim a man of truth, of mercy;
        For, being transported by my jealousies
        To bloody thoughts and to revenge, I chose
        Camillo for the minister to poison
        My friend Polixenes, which had been done,
160   But that the good mind of Camillo tardied
        My swift command, though I with death and with
        Reward did threaten and encourage him,
        Not doing it and being done. He, most humane
        And filled with honor, to my kingly guest
165   Unclasped my practice, quit his fortunes here,
        Which you knew great, and to the hazard
        Of all incertainties himself commended,
        No richer than his honor. How he glisters
        Through my rust! and how his piety
        Does my deeds make the blacker!

                    [Enter Paulina.]

170 *Paulina.*   Woe the while!
        O, cut my lace, lest my heart, cracking it,
        Break too!
        Lord.   What fit is this, good lady?
        Paulina. What studied torments, tyrant, hast for me?
        What wheels? racks? fires? what flaying? boiling
175   In leads or oils? what old or newer torture
        Must I receive, whose every word deserves

165 *Unclasped my practice* revealed my evil design 167 *commended* entrusted
168 *glisters* shines 169 (to regularize the verse, many editors emend
Through to *Thorough*, a common variant) 170 *while* time

To taste of thy most worst? Thy tyranny,
Together working with thy jealousies,
Fancies too weak for boys, too green and idle
For girls of nine, O, think what they have done,   180
And then run mad indeed, stark mad, for all
Thy bygone fooleries were but spices of it.
That thou betrayedst Polixenes, 'twas nothing;
That did but show thee, of a fool, inconstant
And damnable ingrateful. Nor was't much   185
Thou wouldst have poisoned good Camillo's honor,
To have him kill a king—poor trespasses,
More monstrous standing by. Whereof I reckon
The casting forth to crows thy baby daughter
To be or none or little, though a devil   190
Would have shed water out of fire ere done't.
Nor is't directly laid to thee, the death
Of the young prince, whose honorable thoughts,
Thoughts high for one so tender, cleft the heart
That could conceive a gross and foolish sire   195
Blemished his gracious dam. This is not, no,
Laid to thy answer. But the last—O lords,
When I have said, cry 'Woe!'—the queen, the queen,
The sweet'st, dear'st creature's dead, and vengeance for't
Not dropped down yet.
Lord.   The higher powers forbid!   200
Paulina. I say she's dead; I'll swear't. If word nor oath
Prevail not, go and see. If you can bring
Tincture or lustre in her lip, her eye,
Heat outwardly or breath within, I'll serve you
As I would do the gods. But, O thou tyrant,   205
Do not repent these things, for they are heavier

182 *spices* small things 184 *of a fool* for a fool 187 *poor* slight 203 *Tincture . . . eye* color to the lip or brightness to the eye

Than all thy woes can stir. Therefore betake thee
To nothing but despair. A thousand knees
Ten thousand years together, naked, fasting,

210   Upon a barren mountain, and still winter
In storm perpetual, could not move the gods
To look that way thou wert.

Leontes.   Go on, go on.
Thou canst not speak too much. I have deserved
All tongues to talk their bitt'rest.

Lord.   Say no more.

215   Howe'er the business goes, you have made fault
I' th' boldness of your speech.

Paulina.   I am sorry for't.
All faults I make, when I shall come to know them,
I do repent. Alas, I have showed too much
The rashness of a woman. He is touched

220   To the noble heart. What's gone and what's past help
Should be past grief. Do not receive affliction
At my petition. I beseech you, rather
Let me be punished, that have minded you
Of what you should forget. Now, good my liege,

225   Sir, royal sir, forgive a foolish woman.
The love I bore your queen — lo, fool again! —
I'll speak of her no more, nor of your children;
I'll not remember you of my own lord,
Who is lost too. Take your patience to you,
And I'll say nothing.

230 *Leontes.*   Thou didst speak but well
When most the truth, which I receive much better
Than to be pitied of thee. Prithee, bring me
To the dead bodies of my queen and son.

---

207 *stir* alter   212 *look . . . wert* take notice of you   223 *minded* reminded
229 *Take . . . you* be patient

One grave shall be for both. Upon them shall
The causes of their death appear, unto   235
Our shame perpetual. Once a day I'll visit
The chapel where they lie, and tears shed there
Shall be my recreation. So long as nature
Will bear up with this exercise, so long
I daily vow to use it. Come, and lead me   240
Unto these sorrows.   *Exeunt.*

Enter Antigonus, [and] a Mariner, [with a] Babe.   III, iii

Antigonus. Thou art perfect then our ship hath touched upon
    The deserts of Bohemia?
Mariner.   Ay, my lord, and fear
    We have landed in ill time. The skies look grimly
    And threaten present blusters. In my conscience,
    The heavens with that we have in hand are angry   5
    And frown upon's.
Antigonus. Their sacred wills be done! Go, get aboard;
    Look to thy bark. I'll not be long before
    I call upon thee.
Mariner.   Make your best haste, and go not
    Too far i' th' land. 'Tis like to be loud weather.   10
    Besides, this place is famous for the creatures
    Of prey that keep upon't.
Antigonus.   Go thou away;
    I'll follow instantly.
Mariner.   I am glad at heart
    To be so rid o' th' business.   *Exit.*

238 *recreation* refreshing of mind and spirit III, iii, 1 *perfect* sure 4 *conscience* opinion 12 *keep* live

Antigonus.   Come, poor babe.
15   I have heard, but not believed, the spirits o' th' dead
    May walk again. If such thing be, thy mother
    Appeared to me last night, for ne'er was dream
    So like a waking. To me comes a creature,
    Sometimes her head on one side, some another.
20   I never saw a vessel of like sorrow,
    So filled and so becoming. In pure white robes,
    Like very sanctity, she did approach
    My cabin where I lay; thrice bowed before me,
    And, gasping to begin some speech, her eyes
25   Became two spouts. The fury spent, anon
    Did this break her from: 'Good Antigonus,
    Since fate, against thy better disposition,
    Hath made thy person for the thrower-out
    Of my poor babe, according to thine oath,
30   Places remote enough are in Bohemia;
    There weep and leave it crying. And, for the babe
    Is counted lost for ever, Perdita,
    I prithee, call't. For this ungentle business,
    Put on thee by my lord, thou ne'er shalt see
35   Thy wife Paulina more.' And so, with shrieks,
    She melted into air. Affrighted much,
    I did in time collect myself, and thought
    This was so and no slumber. Dreams are toys;
    Yet for this once, yea, superstitiously,
40   I will be squared by this. I do believe
    Hermione hath suffered death, and that
    Apollo would, this being indeed the issue
    Of King Polixenes, it should here be laid,
    Either for life or death, upon the earth

25 *anon* presently   32 *Perdita* i.e. the lost one (feminine)   38 *toys* trifles
39 *superstitiously* punctiliously   40 *squared* ruled

Of its right father. Blossom, speed thee well.   45
There lie, and there thy character; there these,
Which may, if fortune please, both breed thee, pretty,
And still rest thine. The storm begins. Poor wretch,
That for thy mother's fault art thus exposed
To loss and what may follow. Weep I cannot,   50
But my heart bleeds; and most accursed am I
To be by oath enjoined to this. Farewell!
The day frowns more and more. Thou'rt like to have
A lullaby too rough. I never saw
The heavens so dim by day. A savage clamor!   55
Well may I get aboard! This is the chase.
I am gone for ever.   *Exit, pursued by a bear.*

[Enter] Shepherd.

Shepherd. I would there were no age between ten and
three-and-twenty, or that youth would sleep out the rest;
for there is nothing in the between but getting wenches 60
with child, wronging the ancientry, stealing, fighting.
Hark you now. Would any but these boiled brains of
nineteen and two-and-twenty hunt this weather? They
have scared away two of my best sheep, which I fear the
wolf will sooner find than the master. If anywhere I have 65
them, 'tis by the seaside, browsing of ivy. Good luck,
an't be thy will! What have we here? Mercy on's, a
barne, a very pretty barne! A boy or a child, I wonder?
A pretty one, a very pretty one. Sure, some scape.
Though I am not bookish, yet I can read waiting-gentle- 70
woman in the scape. This has been some stair-work, some

46 *character* writing *these* i.e. gold and the jewels by which she is later to
be identified 47 *breed* rear 58 (As ten seems too tender an age to indulge
in some of the escapades referred to, some editors change *ten* to *sixteen.*
If written in Arabic numerals, either 16 or 19 might easily be misread
10. Cf. line 63.) 61 *ancientry* old people 69 *scape* escapade

trunk-work, some behind-door-work. They were
warmer that got this than the poor thing is here. I'll take
it up for pity. Yet I'll tarry till my son come. He hallooed
75 but even now. Whoa, ho, hoa!

Enter Clown.

Clown. Hilloa, loa!

Shepherd. What, art so near? If thou'lt see a thing to talk
on when thou art dead and rotten, come hither. What
ail'st thou, man?

80 *Clown.* I have seen two such sights, by sea and by land —
but I am not to say it is a sea, for it is now the sky; betwixt
the firmament and it you cannot thrust a bodkin's point.

Shepherd. Why, boy, how is it?

Clown. I would you did but see how it chafes, how it rages,
85 how it takes up the shore. But that's not to the point.
O, the most piteous cry of the poor souls! Sometimes to
see 'em, and not to see 'em. Now the ship boring the
moon with her main-mast, and anon swallowed with
yest and froth, as you'ld thrust a cork into a hogshead.
90 And then for the land-service — to see how the bear tore
out his shoulder-bone, how he cried to me for help and
said his name was Antigonus, a nobleman. But to make
an end of the ship — to see how the sea flap-dragoned
it. But, first, how the poor souls roared, and the sea
95 mocked them, and how the poor gentleman roared and
the bear mocked him, both roaring louder than the sea or
weather.

Shepherd. Name of mercy, when was this, boy?

Clown. Now, now; I have not winked since I saw these

72 *trunk-work* a pun on *trunk* meaning (1) a secret place (2) the body apart
from head and limbs 73 *got* begot 76 *Clown* country fellow 89 *yest*
foam 90 *land-service* (1) a dish of food served on land (2) the branch of the
military serving on land, not at sea 93 *flap-dragoned* swallowed whole

sights. The men are not yet cold under water, nor the 100
bear half dined on the gentleman. He's at it now.

Shepherd. Would I had been by, to have helped the old man.

Clown. I would you had been by the ship side, to have
helped her. There your charity would have lacked footing.

Shepherd. Heavy matters, heavy matters! But look thee 105
here, boy. Now bless thyself! thou mettest with things
dying, I with things new-born. Here's a sight for thee.
Look thee, a bearing-cloth for a squire's child. Look thee
here. Take up, take up, boy; open't. So, let's see. It was
told me I should be rich by the fairies. This is some 110
changeling. Open't. What's within, boy?

Clown. You're a made old man. If the sins of your youth
are forgiven you, you're well to live. Gold! all gold!

Shepherd. This is fairy gold, boy, and 'twill prove so. Up
with't, keep it close. Home, home, the next way. We are 115
lucky, boy, and to be so still requires nothing but secrecy.
Let my sheep go. Come, good boy, the next way home.

Clown. Go you the next way with your findings. I'll go
see if the bear be gone from the gentleman and how
much he hath eaten. They are never curst but when they 120
are hungry. If there be any of him left, I'll bury it.

Shepherd. That's a good deed. If thou mayest discern by
that which is left of him what he is, fetch me to the sight
of him.

Clown. Marry, will I; and you shall help to put him i' the 125
ground.

Shepherd. 'Tis a lucky day, boy, and we'll do good deeds
on't.   *Exeunt.*

108 *bearing-cloth* cloth or mantle in which a child is carried to baptism
111 *changeling* child taken or left by fairies   113 *well to live* well-to-do
115 *close* secret   *next* nearest   120 *curst* mean

IV, i   *Enter Time, the Chorus.*

Time. I, that please some, try all, both joy and terror
    Of good and bad, that makes and unfolds error,
    Now take upon me, in the name of Time,
    To use my wings. Impute it not a crime
5   To me or my swift passage that I slide
    O'er sixteen years and leave the growth untried
    Of that wide gap, since it is in my power
    To o'erthrow law and in one self-born hour
    To plant and o'erwhelm custom. Let me pass
10   The same I am, ere ancient'st order was
    Or what is now received. I witness to
    The times that brought them in. So shall I do
    To the freshest things now reigning, and make stale
    The glistering of this present, as my tale
15   Now seems to it. Your patience this allowing,
    I turn my glass and give my scene such growing
    As you had slept between. Leontes leaving,
    The effects of his fond jealousies so grieving
    That he shuts up himself, imagine me,
20   Gentle spectators, that I now may be
    In fair Bohemia. And remember well,
    I mentioned a son o' th' king's, which Florizel
    I now name to you, and with speed so pace
    To speak of Perdita, now grown in grace
25   Equal with wond'ring. What of her ensues

IV, i (Because of its awkwardness in both verse and thought, some editors
have accepted Heath's view that this chorus is an interpolation written by
one other than Shakespeare. Professor Kittredge defends its authenticity,
declaring it written to fit the character of 'Father Time—a doddering,
toothless ancient, halting but fluent, senile but self-assured, ridiculous but
triumphant.') 1 *try* test 1–2 *joy . . . bad* joy to good men and terror to
bad 2 *unfolds* reveals 6 *growth untried* events untold 14 *glistering* brightness 18 *fond* foolish 23 *pace* proceed

I list not prophesy; but let Time's news
Be known when 'tis brought forth. A shepherd's daughter
And what to her adheres, which follows after,
Is th' argument of Time. Of this allow
If ever you have spent time worse ere now;   30
If never, yet that Time himself doth say
He wishes earnestly you never may.   *Exit.*

Enter Polixenes and Camillo.   IV, ii

Polixenes. I pray thee, good Camillo, be no more impor-
tunate. 'Tis a sickness denying thee anything, a death to
grant this.

Camillo. It is fifteen years since I saw my country. Though
I have for the most part been aired abroad, I desire to lay   5
my bones there. Besides, the penitent king, my master,
hath sent for me, to whose feeling sorrows I might be
some allay — or I o'erween to think so — which is another
spur to my departure.

Polixenes. As thou lov'st me, Camillo, wipe not out the rest 10
of thy services by leaving me now. The need I have of
thee thine own goodness hath made. Better not to have
had thee than thus to want thee. Thou, having made me
businesses which none without thee can sufficiently
manage, must either stay to execute them thyself or take   15
away with thee the very services thou hast done, which
if I have not enough considered — as too much I cannot —
to be more thankful to thee shall be my study, and my
profit therein the heaping friendships. Of that fatal coun-

26 *list not* do not wish to 28 *adheres* relates 29 *argument* story IV, ii, 5
been aired lived 8 *o'erween* am presumptuous 13 *want* be without 19
heaping full

20 try, Sicilia, prithee speak no more, whose very naming
punishes me with the remembrance of that penitent, as
thou call'st him, and reconciled king, my brother, whose
loss of his most precious queen and children are even now
to be afresh lamented. Say to me, when saw'st thou the
25 Prince Florizel, my son? Kings are no less unhappy, their
issue not being gracious, than they are in losing them
when they have approved their virtues.

Camillo. Sir, it is three days since I saw the prince. What
his happier affairs may be, are to me unknown, but I have
30 missingly noted he is of late much retired from court and
is less frequent to his princely exercises than formerly he
hath appeared.

Polixenes. I have considered so much, Camillo, and with
some care — so far that I have eyes under my service
35 which look upon his removedness, from whom I have
this intelligence, that he is seldom from the house of a
most homely shepherd, a man, they say, that from very
nothing, and beyond the imagination of his neighbors, is
grown into an unspeakable estate.

40 *Camillo.* I have heard, sir, of such a man, who hath a
daughter of most rare note. The report of her is extended
more than can be thought to begin from such a cottage.

Polixenes. That's likewise part of my intelligence; but, I
fear, the angle that plucks our son thither. Thou shalt
45 accompany us to the place, where we will, not appearing
what we are, have some question with the shepherd, from
whose simplicity I think it not uneasy to get the cause of
my son's resort thither. Prithee be my present partner in
this business, and lay aside the thoughts of Sicilia.

27 *approved* proved   30 *missingly* in missing him   35 *look* spy   36 *intelligence* report   37 *homely* unpretentious   39 *unspeakable estate* untold wealth
44 *angle* fishhook

Camillo. I willingly obey your command.   50
Polixenes. My best Camillo! We must disguise ourselves.
                                        Exeunt.

                Enter Autolycus, singing.   IV, iii

When daffodils begin to peer,
   With heigh! the doxy over the dale,
Why, then comes in the sweet o' the year,
   For the red blood reigns in the winter's pale.

The white sheet bleaching on the hedge,   5
   With heigh! the sweet birds, O how they sing!
Doth set my pugging tooth on edge,
   For a quart of ale is a dish for a king.

The lark, that tirra-lyra chants,
   With heigh! with heigh! the thrush and the jay,   10
Are summer songs for me and my aunts,
   While we lie tumbling in the hay.

I have served Prince Florizel and in my time wore three-
pile, but now I am out of service.

   But shall I go mourn for that, my dear?   15
      The pale moon shines by night.
   And when I wander here and there,
      I then do most go right.

   If tinkers may have leave to live,
      And bear the sow-skin budget,   20

IV, iii, 1 *peer* appear 2 *doxy* female beggar, prostitute 4 *in the winter's
pale* (1) instead of winter's pallor (2) in winter's domain 7 *pugging* pilfer-
ing (?) (cf. sweet tooth) 11 *aunts* i.e. prostitutes 13–14 *three-pile* the
finest velvet 20 *budget* sack

> Then my account I well may give,
> And in the stocks avouch it.

My traffic is sheets; when the kite builds, look to lesser
linen. My father named me Autolycus, who being, as I
25   am, littered under Mercury, was likewise a snapper-up
of unconsidered trifles. With die and drab I purchased
this caparison, and my revenue is the silly cheat. Gallows
and knock are too powerful on the highway; beating
and hanging are terrors to me. For the life to come, I
30   sleep out the thought of it. A prize! a prize!

Enter Clown.

Clown. Let me see; every 'leven wether tods; every tod
yields pound and odd shilling; fifteen hundred shorn,
what comes the wool to?
Autolycus. [aside] If the springe hold, the cock's mine.
35 *Clown.* I cannot do't without counters. Let me see; what
am I to buy for our sheep-shearing feast? Three pound
of sugar, five pound of currants, rice – what will this
sister of mine do with rice? But my father hath made her
mistress of the feast, and she lays it on. She hath made me
40   four and twenty nosegays for the shearers – three-man
songmen all, and very good ones; but they are most of
them means and bases, but one puritan amongst them,
and he sings psalms to hornpipes. I must have saffron to

23 *lesser* smaller pieces of 25 *littered under Mercury* born when the planet
Mercury was in the ascendant (as Mercury was the god of thieving, both
the earlier Autolycus, father of Odysseus, and this his namesake are skilled
in that art) 26–27 *With . . . caparison* by dice and harlots I got this attire
27 *revenue* source of income 30 *prize* booty or one from whom it may be
taken 31 *'leven wether tods* eleven sheep yield a tod (an old weight for
wool) 40–41 *three-man songmen* men who sing catches or rounds 42
means tenors

color the warden pies; mace; dates? — none, that's out of
my note; nutmegs, seven; a race or two of ginger, but 45
that I may beg; four pound of prunes, and as many of
raisins o' the sun.

Autolycus. O that ever I was born! *[Grovels on the ground.]*

Clown. I' the name of me —

Autolycus. O, help me, help me! pluck but off these rags, 50
and then death, death!

Clown. Alack, poor soul, thou hast need of more rags to
lay on thee, rather than have these off.

Autolycus. O, sir, the loathsomeness of them offends me
more than the stripes I have received, which are mighty 55
ones and millions.

Clown. Alas, poor man! A million of beating may come to
a great matter.

Autolycus. I am robbed, sir, and beaten, my money and
apparel ta'en from me, and these detestable things put 60
upon me.

Clown. What, by a horseman, or a footman?

Autolycus. A footman, sweet sir, a footman.

Clown. Indeed, he should be a footman by the garments
he has left with thee. If this be a horseman's coat, it hath 65
seen very hot service. Lend me thy hand, I'll help thee.
Come, lend me thy hand.   *[Helps him up.]*

Autolycus. O, good sir, tenderly. O!

Clown. Alas, poor soul!

Autolycus. O, good sir, softly, good sir. I fear, sir, my 70
shoulder-blade is out.

Clown. How now? canst stand?

Autolycus. *[picking his pocket]* Softly, dear sir; good sir,
softly. You ha' done me a charitable office.

44 *warden* pear   44–45 *that's . . . note* that I am to take no note of   45 *race*
root   47 *o' the sun* sun-dried

75 *Clown.* Dost lack any money? I have a little money for thee.

Autolycus. No, good sweet sir; no, I beseech you, sir. I have
a kinsman not past three quarters of a mile hence, unto
whom I was going. I shall there have money, or anything
I want. Offer me no money, I pray you; that kills my
80 heart.

Clown. What manner of fellow was he that robbed you?

Autolycus. A fellow, sir, that I have known to go about
with troll-my-dames. I knew him once a servant of the
prince. I cannot tell, good sir, for which of his virtues it
85 was, but he was certainly whipped out of the court.

Clown. His vices, you would say. There's no virtue
whipped out of the court. They cherish it to make it stay
there, and yet it will no more but abide.

Autolycus. Vices, I would say, sir. I know this man well.
90 He hath been since an ape-bearer, then a process-server, a
bailiff. Then he compassed a motion of the Prodigal Son,
and married a tinker's wife within a mile where my land
and living lies, and, having flown over many knavish
professions, he settled only in rogue. Some call him Autol-
95 ycus.

Clown. Out upon him! Prig, for my life, prig! He haunts
wakes, fairs, and bear-baitings.

Autolycus. Very true, sir; he, sir, he. That's the rogue that
put me into this apparel.

100 *Clown.* Not a more cowardly rogue in all Bohemia. If you
had but looked big and spit at him, he'ld have run.

Autolycus. I must confess to you, sir, I am no fighter. I am
false of heart that way, and that he knew, I warrant him.

Clown. How do you now?

105 *Autolycus.* Sweet sir, much better than I was. I can stand

83 *troll-my-dames* a game resembling bagatelle   91 *compassed a motion*
devised a puppet-show   96 *Prig* thief

and walk. I will even take my leave of you and pace softly
  towards my kinsman's.
Clown. Shall I bring thee on the way?
Autolycus. No, good-faced sir; no, sweet sir.
Clown. Then fare thee well. I must go buy spices for our 110
  sheep-shearing.
Autolycus. Prosper you, sweet sir.   *Exit [Clown.]*
  Your purse is not hot enough to purchase your spice.
  I'll be with you at your sheep-shearing too. If I make
  not this cheat bring out another and the shearers prove 115
  sheep, let me be unrolled and my name put in the book
  of virtue.

Song.

Jog on, jog on, the foot-path way,
  And merrily hent the stile-a.
A merry heart goes all the day,   120
  Your sad tires in a mile-a.   *Exit.*

Enter Florizel, Perdita.   IV, iv

Florizel. These your unusual weeds to each part of you
  Do give a life—no shepherdess, but Flora
  Peering in April's front. This your sheep-shearing
  Is as a meeting of the petty gods,
  And you the queen on't.
Perdita.   Sir, my gracious lord,
  To chide at your extremes it not becomes me—
  O, pardon, that I name them. Your high self,

116 *unrolled* removed from the roll of thieves   119 *hent* take hold of
IV, iv, 2 *Flora* the goddess of flowers   3 *April's front* early April   6 *extremes* exaggerations

      The gracious mark o' th' land, you have obscured
      With a swain's wearing, and me, poor lowly maid,
10   Most goddess-like pranked up. But that our feasts
      In every mess have folly, and the feeders
      Digest it with a custom, I should blush
      To see you so attired, swoon, I think,
      To show myself a glass.
Florizel.   I bless the time
15   When my good falcon made her flight across
      Thy father's ground.
Perdita.   Now Jove afford you cause!
      To me the difference forges dread; your greatness
      Hath not been used to fear. Even now I tremble
      To think your father, by some accident,
20   Should pass this way as you did. O, the Fates!
      How would he look, to see his work, so noble,
      Vilely bound up? What would he say? Or how
      Should I, in these my borrowed flaunts, behold
      The sternness of his presence?
Florizel.   Apprehend
25   Nothing but jollity. The gods themselves,
      Humbling their deities to love, have taken
      The shapes of beasts upon them. Jupiter
      Became a bull, and bellowed; the green Neptune
      A ram, and bleated; and the fire-robed god,
30   Golden Apollo, a poor humble swain,
      As I seem now. Their transformations
      Were never for a piece of beauty rarer,
      Nor in a way so chaste, since my desires

8 *mark* ornament 9 *wearing* clothes 10 *pranked up* made fine 13 *swoon* (this emendation of the folio *sworn*, first suggested by Theobald, has been widely accepted) 27–30 (Jupiter took the shape of a bull to carry off Europa, Neptune that of a ram to woo Theophane, and Apollo, exiled from heaven by Jupiter, served Admetus as a shepherd and enabled him to win Alcestis)

Run not before mine honor, nor my lusts
Burn hotter than my faith.
Perdita.   O, but, sir,   35
Your resolution cannot hold when 'tis
Opposed, as it must be, by th' power of the king.
One of these two must be necessities,
Which then will speak, that you must change this purpose,
Or I my life.
Florizel.   Thou dearest Perdita,   40
With these forced thoughts, I prithee, darken not
The mirth o' th' feast. Or I'll be thine, my fair,
Or not my father's. For I cannot be
Mine own, nor anything to any, if
I be not thine. To this I am most constant,   45
Though destiny say no. Be merry, gentle;
Strangle such thoughts as these with anything
That you behold the while. Your guests are coming.
Lift up your countenance, as it were the day
Of celebration of that nuptial which   50
We two have sworn shall come.
Perdita.   O lady Fortune,
Stand you auspicious!
Florizel.   See, your guests approach.
Address yourself to entertain them sprightly,
And let's be red with mirth.

[*Enter*] *Shepherd, Clown,* [*with*] *Polixenes* [*and*] *Camillo*
    [*disguised*], *Mopsa, Dorcas, Servants.*

Shepherd. Fie, daughter! When my old wife lived, upon   55
This day she was both pantler, butler, cook,
Both dame and servant; welcomed all, served all;
Would sing her song and dance her turn; now here

41 *forced* far-fetched   42 *Or* either

89

At upper end o' th' table, now i' th' middle;
60   On his shoulder, and his; her face o' fire
With labor, and the thing she took to quench it
She would to each one sip. You are retired,
As if you were a feasted one and not
The hostess of the meeting. Pray you bid
65   These unknown friends to's welcome, for it is
A way to make us better friends, more known.
Come, quench your blushes and present yourself
That which you are, mistress o' th' feast. Come on,
And bid us welcome to your sheep-shearing,
As your good flock shall prosper.

70 *Perdita.*   *[to Polixenes]* Sir, welcome.
It is my father's will I should take on me
The hostess-ship o' th' day. *[to Camillo]* You're welcome,
    sir.
Give me those flowers there, Dorcas. Reverend sirs,
For you there's rosemary and rue; these keep
75   Seeming and savor all the winter long.
Grace and remembrance be to you both,
And welcome to our shearing!

Polixenes.   Shepherdess —
A fair one are you — well you fit our ages
With flowers of winter.

Perdita.   Sir, the year growing ancient,
80   Not yet on summer's death nor on the birth
Of trembling winter, the fairest flowers o' th' season
Are our carnations and streaked gillyvors,
Which some call nature's bastards. Of that kind
Our rustic garden's barren, and I care not
To get slips of them.

74 *rosemary . . . rue* (associated respectively with remembrance and grace)
82 *gillyvors* gillyflowers, clove pinks   83 *nature's bastards* i.e. created by
crossbreeding

Polixenes.   Wherefore, gentle maiden,   85
  Do you neglect them?
Perdita.   For I have heard it said
  There is an art which in their piedness shares
  With great creating nature.
Polixenes.   Say there be;
  Yet nature is made better by no mean
  But nature makes that mean. So, over that art   90
  Which you say adds to nature, is an art
  That nature makes. You see, sweet maid, we marry
  A gentler scion to the wildest stock,
  And make conceive a bark of baser kind
  By bud of nobler race. This is an art   95
  Which does mend nature – change it rather – but
  The art itself is nature.
Perdita.   So it is.
Polixenes. Then make your garden rich in gillyvors,
  And do not call them bastards.
Perdita.   I'll not put
  The dibble in earth to set one slip of them,   100
  No more than, were I painted, I would wish
  This youth should say 'twere well, and only therefore
  Desire to breed by me. Here's flowers for you,
  Hot lavender, mints, savory, marjoram,
  The marigold, that goes to bed wi' th' sun   105
  And with him rises weeping. These are flowers
  Of middle summer, and I think they are given
  To men of middle age. You're very welcome.
Camillo. I should leave grazing, were I of your flock,
  And only live by gazing.

87–88 *There ... nature* i.e. the particolor of the flower owes as much to the
skill of the gardener as to nature   89 *mean* method   100 *dibble* instrument
for making holes for seed

110 *Perdita*. Out, alas!
　　　You'd be so lean that blasts of January
　　　Would blow you through and through. Now, my fair'st
　　　　　friend,
　　　I would I had some flowers o' th' spring that might
　　　Become your time of day, and yours, and yours,
115　That wear upon your virgin branches yet
　　　Your maidenheads growing. O Proserpina,
　　　For the flowers now that, frighted, thou let'st fall
　　　From Dis's wagon; daffodils,
　　　That come before the swallow dares, and take
120　The winds of March with beauty; violets dim,
　　　But sweeter than the lids of Juno's eyes
　　　Or Cytherea's breath; pale primroses,
　　　That die unmarried, ere they can behold
　　　Bright Phoebus in his strength – a malady
125　Most incident to maids; bold oxlips and
　　　The crown imperial; lilies of all kinds,
　　　The flower-de-luce being one. O, these I lack
　　　To make you garlands of, and my sweet friend,
　　　To strew him o'er and o'er!
　　　Florizel. What, like a corse?
130 *Perdita*. No, like a bank for love to lie and play on.
　　　Not like a corse; or if, not to be buried,
　　　But quick and in mine arms. Come, take your flowers.
　　　Methinks I play as I have seen them do
　　　In Whitsun pastorals. Sure this robe of mine
　　　Does change my disposition.

116 *Proserpina* Ceres' daughter, who, spied by Dis (Pluto, god of the underworld) while she was gathering flowers, was seized and taken by him to
the underworld to become his queen　119 *take* charm　121 *Juno* wife of
Jupiter and queen of heaven　122 *Cytherea* Venus　124 *Phoebus* the sun
(Phoebus Apollo the sun god)　129 *corse* corpse　134 *Whitsun pastorals*
plays (or morris dances) presented around Whitsun, the seventh Sunday
after Easter

Florizel.   What you do   135
  Still betters what is done. When you speak, sweet,
  I'ld have you do it ever. When you sing,
  I'ld have you buy and sell so, so give alms,
  Pray so, and for the ord'ring your affairs,
  To sing them too. When you do dance, I wish you   140
  A wave o' th' sea, that you might ever do
  Nothing but that, move still, still so,
  And own no other function. Each your doing,
  So singular in each particular,
  Crowns what you are doing in the present deed,   145
  That all your acts are queens.
Perdita.   O Doricles,
  Your praises are too large. But that your youth,
  And the true blood which peeps so fairly through't,
  Do plainly give you out an unstained shepherd,
  With wisdom I might fear, my Doricles,   150
  You wooed me the false way.
Florizel.   I think you have
  As little skill to fear as I have purpose
  To put you to't. But come; our dance, I pray.
  Your hand, my Perdita. So turtles pair
  That never mean to part.
Perdita.   I'll swear for 'em.   155
Polixenes. This is the prettiest low-born lass that ever
  Ran on the greensward. Nothing she does or seems
  But smacks of something greater than herself,
  Too noble for this place.
Camillo.   He tells her something

143 *Each your doing* everything you do 146 *Doricles* the name assumed by
Florizel in his disguise 148 *so* (not in the folio, but inserted by many
editors in the belief it may have been absorbed in the *s* of *peeps*) 152 *skill*
reason 154 *turtles* turtledoves 158 *greater* of gentler blood

93

160   That makes her blood look out. Good sooth, she is
    The queen of curds and cream.

Clown.   Come on, strike up!

Dorcas. Mopsa must be your mistress. Marry, garlic,
  To mend her kissing with!

Mopsa.   Now, in good time!

Clown. Not a word, a word! We stand upon our manners.

165   Come, strike up!   *[Music.]*

Here a dance of Shepherds and Shepherdesses.

Polixenes. Pray, good shepherd, what fair swain is this
  Which dances with your daughter?

Shepherd. They call him Doricles, and boasts himself
  To have a worthy feeding. But I have it

170   Upon his own report and I believe it;
  He looks like sooth. He says he loves my daughter.
  I think so too, for never gazed the moon
  Upon the water as he'll stand and read
  As 'twere my daughter's eyes; and, to be plain,

175   I think there is not half a kiss to choose
  Who loves another best.

Polixenes.   She dances featly.

Shepherd. So she does anything, though I report it
  That should be silent. If young Doricles
  Do light upon her, she shall bring him that

180   Which he not dreams of.

Enter Servant.

Servant. O master, if you did but hear the pedlar at the door,
  you would never dance again after a tabor and pipe –
  no, the bagpipe could not move you. He sings several

---

160 *blood look out* blush   163 *mend . . . with* escape her unpleasant breath
169 *feeding* land on which sheep feed   171 *like sooth* honest   176 *another*
the other   *featly* nimbly

tunes faster than you'll tell money. He utters them as he
had eaten ballads and all men's ears grew to his tunes.   185

Clown. He could never come better. He shall come in. I
love a ballad but even too well if it be doleful matter
merrily set down, or a very pleasant thing indeed and
sung lamentably.

Servant. He hath songs for man or woman, of all sizes. No   190
milliner can so fit his customers with gloves. He has the
prettiest love-songs for maids, so without bawdry, which
is strange, with such delicate burthens of dildos and fadings, 'Jump her and thump her.' And where some stretch-
mouthed rascal would, as it were, mean mischief and   195
break a foul gap into the matter, he makes the maid to
answer, 'Whoop, do me no harm, good man'; puts him
off, slights him, with 'Whoop, do me no harm, good
man.'

Polixenes. This is a brave fellow.   200

Clown. Believe me, thou talkest of an admirable conceited
fellow. Has he any unbraided wares?

Servant. He hath ribbons of all the colors i' th' rainbow,
points more than all the lawyers in Bohemia can learnedly
handle, though they come to him by the gross — inkles,   205
caddises, cambrics, lawns. Why, he sings 'em over as they
were gods or goddesses. You would think a smock were
a she-angel, he so chants to the sleeve-hand and the work
about the square on't.

Clown. Prithee bring him in, and let him approach singing.   210

Perdita. Forewarn him that he use no scurrilous words in's
tunes.   *[Exit Servant.]*

184 *tell* count   193 *dildo* (a word used as a refrain in ballads) 193–94
fadings burdens of songs   201 *conceited* witty   202 *unbraided* unfaded
204 *points* (1) points in an argument (2) laces to fasten doublet and hose
together   205 *inkles* linen tape   206 *caddises* worsted ribbons   209 *square*
the front upper part of a dress

Clown. You have of these pedlars that have more in them
than you'ld think, sister.

215 *Perdita.* Ay, good brother, or go about to think.

Enter Autolycus, singing.

> Lawn as white as driven snow,
> Cyprus black as e'er was crow,
> Gloves as sweet as damask roses,
> Masks for faces and for noses,
> 220 Bugle bracelet, necklace amber,
> Perfume for a lady's chamber,
> Golden quoifs and stomachers
> For my lads to give their dears,
> Pins and poking-sticks of steel,
> 225 What maids lack from head to heel.
> Come buy of me, come; come buy,
>   come buy.
> Buy, lads, or else your lasses cry.
> Come buy.

Clown. If I were not in love with Mopsa, thou shouldst
230 take no money of me; but being enthralled as I am, it
will also be the bondage of certain ribbons and gloves.

Mopsa. I was promised them against the feast, but they
come not too late now.

Dorcas. He hath promised you more than that, or there be
235 liars.

Mopsa. He hath paid you all he promised you. May be he
has paid you more, which will shame you to give him
again.

213 *You have* there are some 220 *Bugle* bead 222 *quoifs* coifs, head-
dresses 224 *poking-sticks* metal rods used to iron pleats 237–38 *to give
him again* into giving back to him

Clown. Is there no manners left among maids? Will they wear their plackets where they should bear their faces? 240 Is there not milking-time, when you are going to bed, or kiln-hole, to whistle off these secrets, but you must be tittle-tattling before all our guests? 'Tis well they are whispering. Clamor your tongues, and not a word more.

Mopsa. I have done. Come, you promised me a tawdry- 245 lace and a pair of sweet gloves.

Clown. Have I not told thee how I was cozened by the way and lost all my money?

Autolycus. And indeed, sir, there are cozeners abroad; therefore it behoves men to be wary. 250

Clown. Fear not thou, man; thou shalt lose nothing here.

Autolycus. I hope so, sir, for I have about me many parcels of charge.

Clown. What hast here? Ballads?

Mopsa. Pray now, buy some. I love a ballad in print, a life, 255 for then we are sure they are true.

Autolycus. Here's one to a very doleful tune, how a usurer's wife was brought to bed of twenty money-bags at a burthen, and how she longed to eat adders' heads and toads carbonadoed. 260

Mopsa. Is it true, think you?

Autolycus. Very true, and but a month old.

Dorcas. Bless me from marrying a usurer!

Autolycus. Here's the midwife's name to't, one Mistress Tale-porter, and five or six honest wives that were pres- 265 ent. Why should I carry lies abroad?

Mopsa. Pray you now, buy it.

242 *kiln-hole* fireplace   244 *Clamor* stop (?) (It is said to be a technical term of bell-ringing, meaning speed up and stop. Suggested emendations are *clammer* and, recently by Professor Sisson, *clam a'*.)   245 *tawdry* necker-chief   247 *cozened* cheated   253 *charge* value   255 *a life* on my life   260 *carbonadoed* grilled

Clown. Come on, lay it by. And let's first see moe ballads; we'll buy the other things anon.

270 *Autolycus.* Here's another ballad of a fish that appeared upon the coast on Wednesday the fourscore of April, forty thousand fathom above water, and sung this ballad against the hard hearts of maids. It was thought she was a woman and was turned into a cold fish for she would not

275 exchange flesh with one that loved her. The ballad is very pitiful and as true.

Dorcas. Is it true too, think you?

Autolycus. Five justices' hands at it, and witnesses more than my pack will hold.

280 *Clown.* Lay it by too. Another.

Autolycus. This is a merry ballad, but a very pretty one.

Mopsa. Let's have some merry ones.

Autolycus. Why, this is a passing merry one and goes to the tune of 'Two maids wooing a man.' There's scarce a

285 maid westward but she sings it. 'Tis in request, I can tell you.

Mopsa. We can both sing it; if thou'lt bear a part, thou shalt hear. 'Tis in three parts.

Dorcas. We had the tune on't a month ago.

290 *Autolycus.* I can bear my part; you must know 'tis my occupation. Have at it with you.

Song.

Autolycus. Get you hence, for I must go
    Where it fits not you to know.
Dorcas. Whither? *Mopsa.* O, whither? *Dorcas.* Whither?
295 *Mopsa.* It becomes thy oath full well,
    Thou to me thy secrets tell.
Dorcas. Me too; let me go thither.

Mopsa. Or thou goest to th' grange or mill.
Dorcas. If to either, thou dost ill.
Autolycus. Neither. *Dorcas.* What, neither?
      Autolycus. Neither.   300
Dorcas. Thou hast sworn my love to be.
Mopsa. Thou hast sworn it more to me.
      Then whither goest? say, whither?

Clown. We'll have this song out anon by ourselves. My
   father and the gentlemen are in sad talk, and we'll not   305
   trouble them. Come, bring away thy pack after me.
   Wenches, I'll buy for you both. Pedlar, let's have the
   first choice. Follow me, girls.
                              [Exit with Dorcas and Mopsa.]
Autolycus. And you shall pay well for 'em.
                                        [Follows singing.]

                         Song.

         Will you buy any tape,   310
         Or lace for your cape,
         My dainty duck, my dear-a?
            Any silk, any thread,
            Any toys for your head
         Of the new'st and finest, finest wear-a?   315
            Come to the pedlar.
            Money's a medler
         That doth utter all men's ware-a.   *Exit.*

                   [Enter Servant.]

Servant. Master, there is three carters, three shepherds,
   three neatherds, three swineherds, that have made them- 320

298 *grange* farm   305 *sad* serious   318 *utter* sell
                         99

selves all men of hair. They call themselves Saltiers, and
they have a dance which the wenches say is a gallimaufry
of gambols, because they are not in't; but they themselves are o' th' mind, if it be not too rough for some that
325 know little but bowling, it will please plentifully.

Shepherd. Away! we'll none on't. Here has been too much
homely foolery already. I know, sir, we weary you.

Polixenes. You weary those that refresh us. Pray, let's see
these four threes of herdsmen.

330 *Servant.* One three of them, by their own report, sir, hath
danced before the king; and not the worst of the three
but jumps twelve foot and a half by th' squire.

Shepherd. Leave your prating. Since these good men are
pleased, let them come in; but quickly now.

335 *Servant.* Why, they stay at door, sir.   *[Exit.]*

Here a dance of twelve Satyrs.

Polixenes. O, father, you'll know more of that hereafter.
[To Camillo] Is it not too far gone? 'Tis time to part them.
He's simple and tells much. — How now, fair shepherd,
Your heart is full of something that does take
340 Your mind from feasting. Sooth, when I was young
And handed love as you do, I was wont
To load my she with knacks. I would have ransacked
The pedlar's silken treasury and have poured it
To her acceptance. You have let him go
345 And nothing marted with him. If your lass
Interpretation should abuse and call this
Your lack of love or bounty, you were straited

321 *of hair* i.e. wearing skins of animals *Saltiers* i.e. satyrs 322 *gallimaufry* hodgepodge 327 *homely* lacking refinement 330 *One three* one group
of three 332 *squire* square (cf. T-square) 341 *handed* pledged by the hand
345 *marted* traded 347 *straited* hard pressed

For a reply, at least if you make a care
Of happy holding her.

Florizel.   Old sir, I know
She prizes not such trifles as these are.   350
The gifts she looks from me are packed and locked
Up in my heart, which I have given already,
But not delivered. O, hear me breathe my life
Before this ancient sir, who, it should seem,
Hath sometime loved. I take thy hand, this hand   355
As soft as dove's down and as white as it,
Or Ethiopian's tooth, or the fanned snow that's bolted
By th' northern blasts twice o'er.

Polixenes.   What follows this?
How prettily the young swain seems to wash
The hand was fair before! I have put you out.   360
But to your protestation; let me hear
What you profess.

Florizel.   Do, and be witness to't.

Polixenes. And this my neighbor too?

Florizel.   And he, and more
Than he, and men, the earth, the heavens, and all —
That, were I crowned the most imperial monarch,   365
Thereof most worthy, were I the fairest youth
That ever made eye swerve, had force and knowledge
More than was ever man's, I would not prize them
Without her love; for her employ them all;
Commend them and condemn them to her service   370
Or to their own perdition.

Polixenes.   Fairly offered.

Camillo. This shows a sound affection.

Shepherd.   But, my daughter,
Say you the like to him?

348 *care* serious wish   357 *fanned* blown   *bolted* sifted

101

Perdita.   I cannot speak
So well, nothing so well; no, nor mean better.
375 By th' pattern of mine own thoughts I cut out
The purity of his.
Shepherd.   Take hands, a bargain!
And, friends unknown, you shall bear witness to't.
I give my daughter to him and will make
Her portion equal his.
Florizel.   O, that must be
380 I' th' virtue of your daughter. One being dead,
I shall have more than you can dream of yet,
Enough then for your wonder. But, come on,
Contract us 'fore these witnesses.
Shepherd.   Come, your hand;
And, daughter, yours.
Polixenes.   Soft, swain, awhile, beseech you.
Have you a father?
385 *Florizel.*   I have, but what of him?
Polixenes. Knows he of this?
Florizel.   He neither does nor shall.
Polixenes. Methinks a father
Is at the nuptial of his son a guest
That best becomes the table. Pray you once more,
390 Is not your father grown incapable
Of reasonable affairs? Is he not stupid
With age and alt'ring rheums? Can he speak?
    hear?
Know man from man? dispute his own estate?
Lies he not bed-rid? and again does nothing
But what he did being childish?
395 *Florizel.*   No, good sir,

384 *Soft* not so fast   391 *reasonable affairs* affairs requiring reason
393 *dispute* discuss

He has his health and ampler strength indeed
Than most have of his age.
Polixenes.   By my white beard,
  You offer him, if this be so, a wrong
  Something unfilial. Reason my son
  Should choose himself a wife, but as good reason   400
  The father, all whose joy is nothing else
  But fair posterity, should hold some counsel
  In such a business.
Florizel.   I yield all this;
  But for some other reasons, my grave sir,
  Which 'tis not fit you know, I not acquaint   405
  My father of this business.
Polixenes.   Let him know't.
Florizel. He shall not.
Polixenes.   Prithee, let him.
Florizel.   No, he must not.
Shepherd. Let him, my son. He shall not need to grieve
  At knowing of thy choice.
Florizel.   Come, come, he must not.
  Mark our contract.
Polixenes.   Mark your divorce, young sir,   410
                              [Discovers himself.]
  Whom son I dare not call. Thou art too base
  To be acknowledged. Thou a sceptre's heir,
  That thus affect'st a sheep-hook! — Thou old traitor,
  I am sorry that by hanging thee I can
  But shorten thy life one week. — And thou, fresh piece   415
  Of excellent witchcraft, who of force must know
  The royal fool thou cop'st with —
Shepherd.   O, my heart!

399 *Something* somewhat *Reason* it is reasonable 416 *of force* perforce
417 *cop'st with* hast to do with

Polixenes. I'll have thy beauty scratched with briers, and
    made
    More homely than thy state. — For thee, fond boy,
420   If I may ever know thou dost but sigh
    That thou no more shalt see this knack — as never
    I mean thou shalt — we'll bar thee from succession,
    Not hold thee of our blood — no, not our kin —
    Farre than Deucalion off. Mark thou my words.
425   Follow us to the court. — Thou churl, for this time,
    Though full of our displeasure, yet we free thee
    From the dead blow of it. — And you, enchantment,
    Worthy enough a herdsman — yea, him too,
    That makes himself, but for our honor therein,
430   Unworthy thee — if ever henceforth thou
    These rural latches to his entrance open,
    Or hoop his body more with thy embraces,
    I will devise a death as cruel for thee
    As thou art tender to't.   *Exit.*

Perdita.   Even here undone!
435   I was not much afeard; for once or twice
    I was about to speak and tell him plainly
    The selfsame sun that shines upon his court
    Hides not his visage from our cottage but
    Looks on alike. Will't please you, sir, be gone?
440   I told you what would come of this. Beseech you,
    Of your own state take care. This dream of mine —
    Being now awake, I'll queen it no inch farther,
    But milk my ewes and weep.

Camillo.   Why, how now, father?
    Speak ere thou diest.

---

419 *fond* foolish   421 *knack* trifle   424 *Farre* farther   *Deucalion* (according
to Greek mythology this king of Thessaly and his wife were the only
human beings to escape a flood sent by Zeus)   427 *dead* death-dealing

Shepherd.   I cannot speak, nor think,
    Nor dare to know that which I know. O sir,   445
    You have undone a man of fourscore three,
    That thought to fill his grave in quiet, yea,
    To die upon the bed my father died,
    To lie close by his honest bones; but now
    Some hangman must put on my shroud and lay me   450
    Where no priest shovels in dust. O cursèd wretch,
    That knew'st this was the prince, and wouldst adventure
    To mingle faith with him. Undone! undone!
    If I might die within this hour, I have lived
    To die when I desire.   *Exit.*

Florizel.   Why look you so upon me?   455
    I am but sorry, not afeard; delayed,
    But nothing altered. What I was, I am,
    More straining on for plucking back, not following
    My leash unwillingly.

Camillo.   Gracious my lord,
    You know your father's temper. At this time   460
    He will allow no speech, which I do guess
    You do not purpose to him; and as hardly
    Will he endure your sight as yet, I fear.
    Then, till the fury of his highness settle,
    Come not before him.

Florizel.   I not purpose it.   465
    I think Camillo?

Camillo.   Even he, my lord.

Perdita. How often have I told you 'twould be thus?
    How often said my dignity would last
    But till 'twere known!

Florizel.   It cannot fail but by
    The violation of my faith; and then   470
    Let nature crush the sides o' th' earth together

105

And mar the seeds within. Lift up thy looks.
From my succession wipe me, father. I
Am heir to my affection.

Camillo.   Be advised.

475 *Florizel.* I am, and by my fancy. If my reason
Will thereto be obedient, I have reason;
If not, my senses, better pleased with madness,
Do bid it welcome.

Camillo.   This is desperate, sir.

Florizel. So call it, but it does fulfil my vow.

480 I needs must think it honesty. Camillo,
Not for Bohemia nor the pomp that may
Be thereat gleaned, for all the sun sees or
The close earth wombs or the profound seas hide
In unknown fathoms, will I break my oath

485 To this my fair beloved. Therefore, I pray you,
As you have ever been my father's honored
    friend,
When he shall miss me — as, in faith, I mean not
To see him any more — cast your good counsels
Upon his passion. Let myself and fortune

490 Tug for the time to come. This you may know
And so deliver: I am put to sea
With her whom here I cannot hold on shore.
And most opportune to our need I have
A vessel rides fast by, but not prepared

495 For this design. What course I mean to hold
Shall nothing benefit your knowledge, nor
Concern me the reporting.

Camillo.   O my lord,

---

475 *fancy* love   490 *Tug* contend   493 *our* (the folio has *her,* which some
editors keep)   496–97 *Shall . . . reporting* it does not behoove you to know
nor me to say

I would your spirit were easier for advice
Or stronger for your need.

Florizel.   Hark, Perdita. *[Draws her aside.]*
I'll hear you by and by.

Camillo.   He's irremovable,   500
Resolved for flight. Now were I happy if
His going I could frame to serve my turn,
Save him from danger, do him love and honor,
Purchase the sight again of dear Sicilia
And that unhappy king, my master, whom   505
I so much thirst to see.

Florizel.   Now, good Camillo.
I am so fraught with curious business that
I leave out ceremony.

Camillo.   Sir, I think
You have heard of my poor services i' th' love
That I have borne your father?

Florizel.   Very nobly   510
Have you deserved. It is my father's music
To speak your deeds, not little of his care
To have them recompensed as thought on.

Camillo.   Well, my lord,
If you may please to think I love the king
And, through him, what is nearest to him, which is   515
Your gracious self, embrace but my direction.
If your more ponderous and settled project
May suffer alteration, on mine honor,
I'll point you where you shall have such receiving
As shall become your highness, where you may   520
Enjoy your mistress, from the whom, I see,
There's no disjunction to be made but by —
As heavens forfend! — your ruin; marry her,

507 *curious* requiring care   516 *embrace . . . direction* accept my advice

And, with my best endeavors in your absence,

525   Your discontenting father strive to qualify

And bring him up to liking.

Florizel.   How, Camillo,

May this, almost a miracle, be done?

That I may call thee something more than man,

And after that trust to thee.

Camillo.   Have you thought on

A place whereto you'll go?

530 *Florizel.*   Not any yet.

But as th' unthought-on accident is guilty

To what we wildly do, so we profess

Ourselves to be the slaves of chance, and flies

Of every wind that blows.

Camillo.   Then list to me.

535   This follows: if you will not change your purpose

But undergo this flight, make for Sicilia,

And there present yourself and your fair princess,

For so I see she must be, 'fore Leontes.

She shall be habited as it becomes

540   The partner of your bed. Methinks I see

Leontes opening his free arms and weeping

His welcomes forth; asks thee the son forgive-

        ness,

As 'twere i' th' father's person; kisses the hands

Of your fresh princess; o'er and o'er divides him

545   'Twixt his unkindness and his kindness; th' one

He chides to hell and bids the other grow

Faster than thought of time.

Florizel.   Worthy Camillo,

---

525 *qualify* assuage   531–32 *unthought-on . . . do* i.e. his unforeseen discovery by his father is to blame for what he rashly does   541 *free* hospitable

What color for my visitation shall I
Hold up before him?

Camillo.   Sent by the king your father
To greet him and to give him comforts. Sir,   550
The manner of your bearing towards him, with
What you, as from your father, shall deliver,
Things known betwixt us three, I'll write you down,
The which shall point you forth at every sitting
What you must say, that he shall not perceive   555
But that you have your father's bosom there
And speak his very heart.

Florizel.   I am bound to you.
There is some sap in this.

Camillo.   A course more promising
Than a wild dedication of yourselves
To unpathed waters, undreamed shores, most certain   560
To miseries enough; no hope to help you,
But as you shake off one to take another;
Nothing so certain as your anchors, who
Do their best office if they can but stay you
Where you'll be loath to be. Besides, you know   565
Prosperity's the very bond of love,
Whose fresh complexion and whose heart together
Affliction alters.

Perdita.   One of these is true.
I think affliction may subdue the cheek
But not take in the mind.

Camillo.   Yea, say you so?   570
There shall not at your father's house these seven years
Be born another such.

548 *color* pretext   554 *point . . . sitting* guide you at every interview   556
bosom confidence   558 *sap* element essential to life   570 *take in* subdue
571 *these seven years* i.e. for a long time to come (*seven* not to be taken
literally)

Florizel.   My good Camillo,
She is as forward of her breeding as
She is i' th' rear 'our birth.
Camillo.   I cannot say 'tis pity
575   She lacks instructions, for she seems a mistress
To most that teach.
Perdita.   Your pardon, sir. For this
I'll blush you thanks.
Florizel.   My prettiest Perdita!
But O, the thorns we stand upon! Camillo,
Preserver of my father, now of me,
580   The medicine of our house, how shall we do?
We are not furnished like Bohemia's son,
Nor shall appear in Sicilia.
Camillo.   My lord,
Fear none of this. I think you know my fortunes
Do all lie there. It shall be so my care
585   To have you royally appointed as if
The scene you play were mine. For instance, sir,
That you may know you shall not want, one word.
                              [They talk aside.]

                         Enter Autolycus.

Autolycus. Ha, ha, what a fool Honesty is! and Trust, his
sworn brother, a very simple gentleman! I have sold all
590   my trumpery. Not a counterfeit stone, not a ribbon, glass,
pomander, brooch, table-book, ballad, knife, tape, glove,
shoe-tie, bracelet, horn-ring, to keep my pack from
fasting. They throng who should buy first, as if my
trinkets had been hallowed and brought a benediction to

573 *forward of* beyond 574 *'our* of our 575 *instructions* schooling 582
appear i.e. as the king's son 591 *table-book* note-book (cf. Hamlet's tables)

the buyer; by which means I saw whose purse was best in 595
picture, and what I saw, to my good use I remembered.
My clown, who wants but something to be a reasonable
man, grew so in love with the wenches' song that he
would not stir his pettitoes till he had both tune and
words, which so drew the rest of the herd to me that all 600
their other senses stuck in ears. You might have pinched a
placket, it was senseless; 'twas nothing to geld a codpiece
of a purse; I could have filed keys off that hung in chains.
No hearing, no feeling, but my sir's song and admiring
the nothing of it. So that in this time of lethargy I picked 605
and cut most of their festival purses; and had not the old
man come in with a whoo-bub against his daughter and
the king's son and scared my choughs from the chaff, I
had not left a purse alive in the whole army.

        [Camillo, Florizel, and Perdita come forward.]

Camillo. Nay, but my letters, by this means being there 610
  So soon as you arrive, shall clear that doubt.
Florizel. And those that you'll procure from King Leontes —
Camillo. Shall satisfy your father.
Perdita.   Happy be you!
  All that you speak shows fair.
Camillo.   *[seeing Autolycus]* Who have we here?
  We'll make an instrument of this, omit 615
  Nothing may give us aid.
Autolycus. If they have overheard me now, why, hanging.
Camillo. How now, good fellow? Why shak'st thou so?
  Fear not, man; here's no harm intended to thee.

595–96 *was best in picture* looked best   599 *pettitoes* toes (usually of a pig)
601 *stuck in ears* were devoted to listening   602 *senseless* without feeling
602–3 *geld . . . purse* remove a purse from a pocket   603 *could* (the folio
has *would*)   604 *my sir's* i.e. the clown's   608 *choughs* birds of the crow
family

620 *Autolycus.* I am a poor fellow, sir.

    Camillo. Why, be so still; here's nobody will steal that from
    thee. Yet for the outside of thy poverty we must make an
    exchange. Therefore discase thee instantly — thou must
    think there's a necessity in't — and change garments with
625   this gentleman. Though the pennyworth on his side be the
    worst, yet hold thee, there's some boot.

    Autolycus. I am a poor fellow, sir. *[aside]* I know ye well
    enough.

    Camillo. Nay, prithee, dispatch. The gentleman is half
630   flayed already.

    Autolycus. Are you in earnest, sir? *[aside]* I smell the trick
    on't.

    Florizel. Dispatch, I prithee.

    Autolycus. Indeed, I have had earnest, but I cannot with
635   conscience take it.

    Camillo. Unbuckle, unbuckle.

                  [Florizel and Autolycus exchange garments.]
    Fortunate mistress — let my prophecy
    Come home to ye! — you must retire yourself
    Into some covert. Take your sweetheart's hat
640   And pluck it o'er your brows, muffle your face,
    Dismantle you, and, as you can, disliken
    The truth of your own seeming, that you may —
    For I do fear eyes over — to shipboard
    Get undescried.

    Perdita.   I see the play so lies
    That I must bear a part.

622 *the outside . . . poverty* thy rags 623 *discase* undress 625–26 *Though . . .
worst* though he gets the worse in the exchange 626 *boot* something additional (usually to equalize an exchange) 629 *dispatch* make haste 630
flayed skinned 634 *earnest* partial prepayment 638 *Come . . . ye* be fulfilled 641–42 *as . . . seeming* as far as you can, alter your true appearance
643 *eyes over* spying

Camillo.   No remedy.   645
  Have you done there?
Florizel.   Should I now meet my father,
  He would not call me son.
Camillo.   Nay, you shall have no hat.
                                    [Gives it to Perdita.]
  Come, lady, come. Farewell, my friend.
Autolycus.   Adieu, sir.
Florizel. O Perdita, what have we twain forgot?
  Pray you, a word.   650
Camillo. *[aside]* What I do next, shall be to tell the
      king
  Of this escape and whither they are bound;
  Wherein my hope is I shall so prevail
  To force him after; in whose company
  I shall review Sicilia, for whose sight   655
  I have a woman's longing.
Florizel.   Fortune speed us!
  Thus we set on, Camillo, to the seaside.
Camillo. The swifter speed the better.
                      Exeunt [Florizel, Perdita, and Camillo].
Autolycus. I understand the business, I hear it. To have an
  open ear, a quick eye, and a nimble hand is necessary for a   660
  cutpurse. A good nose is requisite also, to smell out work
  for the other senses. I see this is the time that the unjust
  man doth thrive. What an exchange had this been without boot! What a boot is here with this exchange! Sure
  the gods do this year connive at us, and we may do any   665
  thing extempore. The prince himself is about a piece of
  iniquity, stealing away from his father with his clog at his
  heels. If I thought it were a piece of honesty to acquaint
  the king withal, I would not do't. I hold it the more

667 *clog* anything which impedes movement

670 knavery to conceal it, and therein am I constant to my
profession.

Enter Clown and Shepherd.

Aside, aside! Here is more matter for a hot brain. Every
lane's end, every shop, church, session, hanging, yields a
careful man work.

675 *Clown.* See, see! What a man you are now! There is no
other way but to tell the king she's a changeling and none
of your flesh and blood.

Shepherd. Nay, but hear me.

Clown. Nay, but hear me.

680 *Shepherd.* Go to, then.

Clown. She being none of your flesh and blood, your flesh
and blood has not offended the king, and so your flesh
and blood is not to be punished by him. Show those
things you found about her, those secret things, all but

685 what she has with her. This being done, let the law go
whistle. I warrant you.

Shepherd. I will tell the king all, every word – yea, and his
son's pranks too, who, I may say, is no honest man,
neither to his father nor to me, to go about to make me

690 the king's brother-in-law.

Clown. Indeed, brother-in-law was the farthest off you
could have been to him, and then your blood had been
the dearer by I know how much an ounce.

Autolycus. [*aside*] Very wisely, puppies.

695 *Shepherd.* Well, let us to the king. There is that in this
fardel will make him scratch his beard.

Autolycus. [*aside*] I know not what impediment this complaint may be to the flight of my master.

676 *changeling* a child left (by fairies) with other than its true parents
680 *Go to* go on   693 *dearer* of greater worth   696 *fardel* bundle

Clown. Pray heartily he be at the palace.

Autolycus. [aside] Though I am not naturally honest, I am 700
so sometimes by chance. Let me pocket up my pedlar's
excrement. [*Takes off his false beard.*] How now, rustics,
whither are you bound?

Shepherd. To the palace, an it like your worship.

Autolycus. Your affairs there, what, with whom, the con- 705
dition of that fardel, the place of your dwelling, your
names, your ages, of what having, breeding, and anything that is fitting to be known, discover.

Clown. We are but plain fellows, sir.

Autolycus. A lie! You are rough and hairy. Let me have no 710
lying. It becomes none but tradesmen, and they often
give us soldiers the lie; but we pay them for it with
stamped coin, not stabbing steel; therefore they do not
give us the lie.

Clown. Your worship had like to have given us one, if you 715
had not taken yourself with the manner.

Shepherd. Are you a courtier, an't like you, sir?

Autolycus. Whether it like me or no, I am a courtier. Seest
thou not the air of the court in these enfoldings? Hath
not my gait in it the measure of the court? Receives not 720
thy nose court-odor from me? Reflect I not on thy baseness court-contempt? Thinkest thou, for that I insinuate,
or toaze from thee thy business, I am therefore no courtier? I am courtier cap-a-pe, and one that will either push
on or pluck back thy business there. Whereupon I com- 725
mand thee to open thy affair.

Shepherd. My business, sir, is to the king.

Autolycus. What advocate hast thou to him?

702 *excrement* appendage   704 *an it like* if it please   707 *having* property
708 *discover* reveal   716 *taken . . . manner* caught yourself in the act (?)
719 *enfoldings* clothes   723 *toaze* tear   724 *cap-a-pe* from head to foot

Shepherd. I know not, an't like you.

730 *Clown.* Advocate's the court-word for a pheasant. Say you
have none.

Shepherd. None, sir. I have no pheasant, cock nor hen.

Autolycus. How blessed are we that are not simple men!
Yet nature might have made me as these are;

735   Therefore I will not disdain.

Clown. This cannot be but a great courtier.

Shepherd. His garments are rich, but he wears them not
handsomely.

Clown. He seems to be the more noble in being fantastical.

740   A great man, I'll warrant. I know by the picking on's
teeth.

Autolycus. The fardel there? What's i' the fardel? Wherefore that box?

Shepherd. Sir, there lies such secrets in this fardel and box,

745   which none must know but the king, and which he shall
know within this hour if I may come to the speech of
him.

Autolycus. Age, thou hast lost thy labor.

Shepherd. Why, sir?

750 *Autolycus.* The king is not at the palace. He is gone aboard
a new ship to purge melancholy and air himself, for, if
thou beest capable of things serious, thou must know the
king is full of grief.

Shepherd. So 'tis said, sir – about his son, that should have

755   married a shepherd's daughter.

Autolycus. If that shepherd be not in hand-fast, let him fly.
The curses he shall have, the tortures he shall feel, will
break the back of man, the heart of monster.

730 *pheasant* i.e. as a bribe to the judge (the clown confuses the two kinds
of courts)   740–41 *picking on's teeth* (picking the teeth was an affectation
of would-be gallants)   756 *hand-fast* custody

Clown. Think you so, sir?

Autolycus. Not he alone shall suffer what wit can make 760
heavy and vengeance bitter; but those that are germane
to him, though removed fifty times, shall all come under
the hangman, which, though it be great pity, yet it is
necessary. An old sheep-whistling rogue, a ram-tender, to
offer to have his daughter come into grace! Some say he 765
shall be stoned, but that death is too soft for him, say I.
Draw our throne into a sheep-cote! All deaths are too few,
the sharpest too easy.

Clown. Has the old man e'er a son, sir, do you hear, an't
like you, sir? 770

Autolycus. He has a son, who shall be flayed alive; then
'nointed over with honey, set on the head of a wasp's
nest; then stand till he be three quarters and a dram dead;
then recovered again with aqua-vitae or some other hot
infusion. Then, raw as he is, and in the hottest day prog- 775
nostication proclaims, shall he be set against a brick-wall,
the sun looking with a southward eye upon him, where
he is to behold him with flies blown to death. But what
talk we of these traitorly rascals, whose miseries are to be
smiled at, their offenses being so capital? Tell me, for 780
you seem to be honest plain men, what you have to the
king. Being something gently considered, I'll bring you
where he is aboard, tender your persons to his presence,
whisper him in your behalfs; and if it be in man besides
the king to effect your suits, here is man shall do it. 785

Clown. He seems to be of great authority. Close with him,
give him gold; and though authority be a stubborn bear,

---

765 *grace* honor   774 *aqua-vitae* brandy   775–76 *prognostication* forecast
(forecasts for the coming year were published annually)   782 *something . . .
considered* given some consideration, i.e. bribe   786 *Close* come to an agreement

yet he is oft led by the nose with gold. Show the inside of
your purse to the outside of his hand, and no more ado.

790   Remember 'stoned,' and 'flayed alive.'

Shepherd. An't please you, sir, to undertake the business for
us, here is that gold I have. I'll make it as much more and
leave this young man in pawn till I bring it you.

Autolycus. After I have done what I promised?

795 *Shepherd.* Ay, sir.

Autolycus. Well, give me the moiety. Are you a party in
this business?

Clown. In some sort, sir. But though my case be a pitiful
one, I hope I shall not be flayed out of it.

800 *Autolycus.* O, that's the case of the shepherd's son. Hang
him, he'll be made an example.

Clown. Comfort, good comfort! We must to the king and
show our strange sights. He must know 'tis none of your
daughter nor my sister; we are gone else. Sir, I will give

805   you as much as this old man does when the business is
performed, and remain, as he says, your pawn till it be
brought you.

Autolycus. I will trust you. Walk before toward the seaside.
Go on the right hand. I will but look upon the hedge and

810   follow you.

Clown. We are blest in this man, as I may say, even blest.

Shepherd. Let's before as he bids us. He was provided to do
us good.   [*Exeunt Shepherd and Clown.*]

Autolycus. If I had a mind to be honest, I see Fortune would

815   not suffer me; she drops booties in my mouth. I am
courted now with a double occasion, gold and a means
to do the prince my master good, which who knows how
that may turn back to my advancement? I will bring

796 *moiety* half   798 *case* (1) position 'in this business' (2) skin   816
courted . . . with tempted . . . by   818 *turn back* revert

these two moles, these blind ones, aboard him. If he think
it fit to shore them again and that the complaint they   820
have to the king concerns him nothing, let him call me
rogue for being so far officious, for I am proof against
that title and what shame else belongs to't. To him will I
present them; there may be matter in it.   *Exit.*

Enter Leontes, Cleomenes, Dion, Paulina, Servants.   V, i

Cleomenes. Sir, you have done enough, and have performed
    A saint-like sorrow. No fault could you make
    Which you have not redeemed — indeed, paid down
    More penitence than done trespass. At the last,
    Do as the heavens have done, forget your evil;   5
    With them forgive yourself.
Leontes.   Whilst I remember
    Her and her virtues, I cannot forget
    My blemishes in them, and so still think of
    The wrong I did myself, which was so much
    That heirless it hath made my kingdom and   10
    Destroyed the sweet'st companion that e'er man
    Bred his hopes out of.
Paulina.   True, too true, my lord.
    If one by one you wedded all the world,
    Or from the all that are took something good
    To make a perfect woman, she you killed   15
    Would be unparalleled.
Leontes.   I think so. Killed?
    She I killed? I did so, but thou strik'st me

819 *aboard him* to him aboard (the ship) V, i, 12 (in the folio the first
True is part of the preceding speech of Leontes)

Sorely to say I did. It is as bitter
Upon thy tongue as in my thought. Now, good now,
Say so but seldom.

20 *Cleomenes.*   Not at all, good lady.
You might have spoken a thousand things that would
Have done the time more benefit and graced
Your kindness better.

Paulina.   You are one of those
Would have him wed again.

Dion.   If you would not so,
25 You pity not the state nor the remembrance
Of his most sovereign name, consider little
What dangers, by his highness' fail of issue,
May drop upon his kingdom and devour
Incertain lookers on. What were more holy
30 Than to rejoice the former queen is well?
What holier than, for royalty's repair,
For present comfort and for future good,
To bless the bed of majesty again
With a sweet fellow to't?

Paulina.   There is none worthy,
35 Respecting her that's gone. Besides, the gods
Will have fulfilled their secret purposes;
For has not the divine Apollo said,
Is't not the tenor of his oracle,
That King Leontes shall not have an heir
40 Till his lost child be found? Which that it shall
Is all as monstrous to our human reason
As my Antigonus to break his grave
And come again to me, who, on my life,
Did perish with the infant. 'Tis your counsel

19 *good now* i.e. I pray you (?) (cf. *Hamlet* I, i, 70) 22 *graced* befitted
29 *Incertain* confused (as to an heir to the throne) 41 *monstrous* incredible

My lord should to the heavens be contrary,   45
Oppose against their wills. *[to Leontes]* Care not for issue;
The crown will find an heir. Great Alexander
Left his to th' worthiest; so his successor
Was like to be the best.

Leontes.   Good Paulina,
Who hast the memory of Hermione,   50
I know, in honor, O that ever I
Had squared me to thy counsel! Then even now
I might have looked upon my queen's full eyes,
Have taken treasure from her lips —

Paulina.   And left them
More rich for what they yielded.

Leontes.   Thou speak'st truth.   55
No more such wives; therefore, no wife! One worse,
And better used, would make her sainted spirit
Again possess her corpse, and on this stage
(Where we offenders now) appear soul-vexed,
And begin, 'Why to me?'

Paulina.   Had she such power,   60
She had just cause.

Leontes.   She had, and would incense me
To murder her I married.

Paulina.   I should so.
Were I the ghost that walked, I'ld bid you mark
Her eye, and tell me for what dull part in't
You chose her. Then I'ld shriek, that even your ears   65
Should rift to hear me, and the words that followed
Should be 'Remember mine.'

52 *squared me to* acted in accordance with 56 *No more* there are no more
59 (The folio includes *appear* within the parentheses. Other changes
which have been suggested include *we're* for *we, move* for *now, offend* as
for *offenders*.)

Leontes.   Stars, stars,
  And all eyes else dead coals! Fear thou no wife;
  I'll have no wife, Paulina.
Paulina.   Will you swear
70 Never to marry but by my free leave?
Leontes. Never, Paulina, so be blest my spirit.
Paulina. Then, good my lords, bear witness to his oath.
Cleomenes. You tempt him overmuch.
Paulina.   Unless another,
  As like Hermione as is her picture,
  Affront his eye.
Cleomenes.   Good madam —
75 *Paulina.*   I have done.
  Yet, if my lord will marry — if you will, sir,
  No remedy but you will — give me the office
  To choose you a queen. She shall not be so young
  As was your former, but she shall be such
80 As, walked your first queen's ghost, it should take joy
  To see her in your arms.
Leontes.   My true Paulina,
  We shall not marry till thou bid'st us.
Paulina.   That
  Shall be when your first queen's again in breath.
  Never till then.

Enter a Servant.

85 *Servant.* One that gives out himself Prince Florizel,
  Son of Polixenes, with his princess — she
  The fairest I have yet beheld — desires access
  To your high presence.
Leontes.   What with him? He comes not

73 *tempt* urge 75 *Affront* confront

Like to his father's greatness. His approach,
So out of circumstance and sudden, tells us   90
'Tis not a visitation framed, but forced
By need and accident. What train?
Servant.   But few,
    And those but mean.
Leontes.   His princess, say you, with him?
Servant. Ay, the most peerless piece of earth, I think,
    That e'er the sun shone bright on.
Paulina.   O Hermione.   95
    As every present time doth boast itself
    Above a better gone, so must thy grave
    Give way to what's seen now. Sir, you yourself
    Have said and writ so, but your writing now
    Is colder than that theme. She had not been,   100
    Nor was not to be equalled — thus your verse
    Flowed with her beauty once. 'Tis shrewdly ebbed
    To say you have seen a better.
Servant.   Pardon, madam.
    The one I have almost forgot — your pardon;
    The other, when she has obtained your eye,   105
    Will have your tongue too. This is a creature,
    Would she begin a sect, might quench the zeal
    Of all professors else, make proselytes
    Of who she but bid follow.
Paulina.   How? not women?
Servant. Women will love her that she is a woman   110
    More worth than any man; men, that she is
    The rarest of all women.
Leontes.   Go, Cleomenes.
    Yourself, assisted with your honored friends,

---

89 *approach* coming   90 *out of circumstance* without formality   91 *framed*
premeditated   108 *professors else* those who profess other faiths

Bring them to our embracement.

Exit [Cleomenes with others].

Still, 'tis strange

He thus should steal upon us.

115 *Paulina.*   Had our prince,
Jewel of children, seen this hour, he had paired
Well with this lord. There was not full a month
Between their births.

Leontes.   Prithee, no more; cease. Thou know'st
He dies to me again when talked of. Sure,
120 When I shall see this gentleman, thy speeches
Will bring me to consider that which may
Unfurnish me of reason. They are come.

Enter Florizel, Perdita, Cleomenes, and others.

Your mother was most true to wedlock, prince,
For she did print your royal father off,
125 Conceiving you. Were I but twenty-one,
Your father's image is so hit in you,
His very air, that I should call you brother,
As I did him, and speak of something wildly
By us performed before. Most dearly welcome!
130 And your fair princess — goddess! O, alas!
I lost a couple that 'twixt heaven and earth
Might thus have stood begetting wonder as
You, gracious couple, do. And then I lost —
All mine own folly — the society,
135 Amity too, of your brave father, whom,
Though bearing misery, I desire my life
Once more to look on him.

Florizel.   By his command
Have I here touched Sicilia, and from him
Give you all greetings that a king, at friend,

122 *Unfurnish* deprive   139 *at friend* in friendship

Can send his brother; and, but infirmity   140
Which waits upon worn times hath something seized
His wished ability, he had himself
The lands and waters 'twixt your throne and his
Measured to look upon you, whom he loves —
He bade me say so — more than all the sceptres   145
And those that bear them living.

Leontes.   O my brother,
Good gentleman, the wrongs I have done thee stir
Afresh within me, and these thy offices,
So rarely kind, are as interpreters
Of my behindhand slackness. Welcome hither,   150
As is the spring to the earth. And hath he too
Exposed this paragon to th' fearful usage,
At least ungentle, of the dreadful Neptune,
To greet a man not worth her pains, much less
Th' adventure of her person?

Florizel.   Good my lord,   155
She came from Libya.

Leontes.   Where the warlike Smalus,
That noble honored lord, is feared and loved?

Florizel. Most royal sir, from thence, from him, whose
    daughter
His tears proclaimed his, parting with her. Thence,
A prosperous south-wind friendly, we have crossed,   160
To execute the charge my father gave me
For visiting your highness. My best train
I have from your Sicilian shores dismissed,
Who for Bohemia bend, to signify
Not only my success in Libya, sir,   165

141 *waits . . . times* accompanies old age *something seized* somewhat taken
away 144 *Measured* journeyed over 148 *offices* courtesies 149–50 *are . . .
slackness* emphasize my tardy, inadequate action 155 *adventure* risk

But my arrival and my wife's in safety
Here where we are.

Leontes.   The blessèd gods
Purge all infection from our air whilst you
Do climate here! You have a holy father,

170 A graceful gentleman, against whose person,
So sacred as it is, I have done sin,
For which the heavens, taking angry note,
Have left me issueless; and your father's blest,
As he from heaven merits it, with you,

175 Worthy his goodness. What might I have been,
Might I a son and daughter now have looked on,
Such goodly things as you?

Enter a Lord.

Lord.   Most noble sir,
That which I shall report will bear no credit,
Were not the proof so nigh. Please you, great sir,

180 Bohemia greets you from himself by me,
Desires you to attach his son, who has –
His dignity and duty both cast off –
Fled from his father, from his hopes, and with
A shepherd's daughter.

Leontes.   Where's Bohemia? Speak.

185 *Lord.* Here in your city. I now came from him.
I speak amazedly, and it becomes
My marvel and my message. To your court
Whiles he was hastening – in the chase, it seems,
Of this fair couple – meets he on the way

190 The father of this seeming lady and

169 *climate* dwell   170 *graceful* gracious   181 *attach* arrest   186 *amazedly*
confusedly   186–87 *it . . . marvel* my confused speech suits (results from)
my wonder   188 *chase* pursuit

Her brother, having both their country quitted
With this young prince.

Florizel.   Camillo has betrayed me,
Whose honor and whose honesty till now
Endured all weathers.

Lord.   Lay't so to his charge.
He's with the king your father.

Leontes.   Who? Camillo?   195

Lord. Camillo, sir. I spake with him, who now
Has these poor men in question. Never saw I
Wretches so quake. They kneel, they kiss the earth,
Forswear themselves as often as they speak.
Bohemia stops his ears, and threatens them   200
With divers deaths in death.

Perdita.   O my poor father!
The heaven sets spies upon us, will not have
Our contract celebrated.

Leontes.   You are married?

Florizel. We are not, sir, nor are we like to be.
The stars, I see, will kiss the valleys first;   205
The odds for high and low's alike.

Leontes.   My lord,
Is this the daughter of a king?

Florizel.   She is
When once she is my wife.

Leontes. That 'once,' I see by your good father's speed,
Will come on very slowly. I am sorry,   210
Most sorry, you have broken from his liking
Where you were tied in duty, and as sorry
Your choice is not so rich in worth as beauty,
That you might well enjoy her.

201 *deaths in death* tortures 206 *odds . . . alike* high and low are alike
subject to misfortune 213 *worth* high birth

Florizel.   Dear, look up.
215 Though Fortune, visible an enemy,
Should chase us with my father, power no jot
Hath she to change our loves. Beseech you, sir,
Remember since you owed no more to time
Than I do now. With thought of such affections,
220 Step forth mine advocate. At your request
My father will grant precious things as trifles.
Leontes. Would he do so, I'ld beg your precious mistress,
Which he counts but a trifle.
Paulina.   Sir, my liege,
Your eye hath too much youth in't. Not a month
225 'Fore your queen died, she was more worth such gazes
Than what you look on now.
Leontes.   I thought of her
Even in these looks I made. *[to Florizel]* But your petition
Is yet unanswered. I will to your father.
Your honor not o'erthrown by your desires,
230 I am a friend to them and you. Upon which errand
I now go toward him; therefore follow me
And mark what way I make. Come, good my lord.
                                        Exeunt.

V, ii   *Enter Autolycus and a Gentleman.*

Autolycus. Beseech you, sir, were you present at this relation?
  1. Gentleman. I was by at the opening of the fardel, heard the
old shepherd deliver the manner how he found it; where-
5 upon, after a little amazedness, we were all commanded

215 *visible* clearly   218–19 *since . . . now* when you were my age   229
Your . . . desires if your desires have not led you to do what is dishonorable
232 *way* progress

out of the chamber. Only this methought I heard the
shepherd say, he found the child.

Autolycus. I would most gladly know the issue of it.

1. *Gentleman.* I make a broken delivery of the business;
but the changes I perceived in the king and Camillo were 10
very notes of admiration. They seemed almost, with
staring on one another, to tear the cases of their eyes.
There was speech in their dumbness, language in their very
gesture. They looked as they had heard of a world ran-
somed, or one destroyed. A notable passion of wonder 15
appeared in them. But the wisest beholder, that knew no
more but seeing, could not say if the importance were joy
or sorrow; but in the extremity of the one, it must needs
be.

Enter another Gentleman.

Here comes a gentleman that haply knows more. The 20
news, Rogero?

2. *Gentleman.* Nothing but bonfires. The oracle is fulfilled;
the king's daughter is found. Such a deal of wonder is
broken out within this hour that ballad-makers cannot be
able to express it. 25

Enter another Gentleman.

Here comes the Lady Paulina's steward; he can deliver
you more. How goes it now, sir? This news which is
called true is so like an old tale that the verity of it is in
strong suspicion. Has the king found his heir?

3. *Gentleman.* Most true, if ever truth were pregnant by 30
circumstance. That which you hear you'll swear you see,

V, ii, 9 *make . . . delivery* give a fragmentary account 11 *admiration* wonder
15 *passion* emotion 17 *seeing* what he saw *importance* import 20 *haply*
perhaps 26 *deliver* tell 30-31 *pregnant by circumstance* obvious from the
evidence

there is such unity in the proofs. The mantle of Queen
Hermione's, her jewel about the neck of it, the letters of
Antigonus found with it, which they know to be his char-
35 acter, the majesty of the creature in resemblance of the
mother, the affection of nobleness which nature shows
above her breeding, and many other evidences proclaim
her with all certainty to be the king's daughter. Did you
see the meeting of the two kings?

40 *2. Gentleman.* No.

3. Gentleman. Then have you lost a sight which was to be
seen, cannot be spoken of. There might you have beheld
one joy crown another, so and in such manner that it
seemed sorrow wept to take leave of them, for their joy
45 waded in tears. There was casting up of eyes, holding up
of hands, with countenance of such distraction that they
were to be known by garment, not by favor. Our king,
being ready to leap out of himself for joy of his found
daughter, as if that joy were now become a loss, cries, 'O,
50 thy mother, thy mother!' then asks Bohemia forgiveness;
then embraces his son-in-law; then again worries he his
daughter with clipping her; now he thanks the old
shepherd, which stands by like a weather-bitten conduit
of many kings' reigns. I never heard of such another en-
55 counter, which lames report to follow it and undoes description to do it.

2. Gentleman. What, pray you, became of Antigonus, that
carried hence the child?

3. Gentleman. Like an old tale still, which will have matter
60 to rehearse, though credit be asleep and not an ear open.

---

32 *unity* agreement   34-35 *character* handwriting   36 *affection of* natural
tendency toward   47 *favor* features   52 *clipping* embracing   53 *conduit*
structure from which flows water (here tears)   55-56 *undoes . . . it* renders
description incapable of describing

He was torn to pieces with a bear. This avouches the shepherd's son, who has not only his innocence, which seems much, to justify him, but a handkerchief and rings of his that Paulina knows.

1. Gentleman. What became of his bark and his followers? 65

3. Gentleman. Wrecked the same instant of their master's death and in the view of the shepherd; so that all the instruments which aided to expose the child were even then lost when it was found. But O, the noble combat that 'twixt joy and sorrow was fought in Paulina! She 70 had one eye declined for the loss of her husband, another elevated that the oracle was fulfilled. She lifted the princess from the earth, and so locks her in embracing as if she would pin her to her heart that she might no more be in danger of losing. 75

1. Gentleman. The dignity of this act was worth the audience of kings and princes, for by such was it acted.

3. Gentleman. One of the prettiest touches of all, and that which angled for mine eyes, caught the water though not the fish, was when, at the relation of the queen's death, 80 with the manner how she came to 't bravely confessed and lamented by the king, how attentiveness wounded his daughter, till, from one sign of dolor to another, she did, with an 'Alas,' I would fain say, bleed tears, for I am sure my heart wept blood. Who was most marble there 85 changed color; some swooned, all sorrowed. If all the world could have seen 't, the woe had been universal.

1. Gentleman. Are they returned to the court?

3. Gentleman. No. The princess, hearing of her mother's statue, which is in the keeping of Paulina — a piece many 90 years in doing and now newly performed by that rare

61 *with* by 62 *innocence* simplicity 82 *attentiveness* i.e. 'the hearing of it' (Wilson) 91 *performed* finished

Italian master, Julio Romano, who, had he himself
eternity and could put breath into his work, would be-
guile Nature of her custom, so perfectly he is her ape. He
95   so near to Hermione hath done Hermione that they say
one would speak to her and stand in hope of answer.
Thither with all greediness of affection are they gone, and
there they intend to sup.

2. Gentleman. I thought she had some great matter there in
100   hand, for she hath privately twice or thrice a day, ever
since the death of Hermione, visited that removed house.
Shall we thither and with our company piece the re-
joicing?

1. Gentleman. Who would be thence that has the benefit
105   of access? Every wink of an eye some new grace will be
born. Our absence makes us unthrifty to our knowledge.
Let's along.   *Exeunt [Gentlemen].*

Autolycus. Now, had I not the dash of my former life in me,
would preferment drop on my head. I brought the old
110   man and his son aboard the prince, told him I heard
them talk of a fardel and I know not what. But he at that
time, over-fond of the shepherd's daughter – so he then
took her to be – who began to be much seasick, and
himself little better, extremity of weather continuing,
115   this mystery remained undiscovered. But 'tis all one to
me; for had I been the finder out of this secret, it would
not have relished among my other discredits.

Enter Shepherd and Clown.

Here come those I have done good to against my will,
and already appearing in the blossoms of their fortune.

92 *Romano* an Italian painter and sculptor who died in 1546   93–94 *be-
guile . . . custom* rob Nature of her business, i.e. creating living people
94 *her ape* Nature's imitator   102 *piece* add to   117 *relished* added relish

Shepherd. Come, boy. I am past moe children, but thy 120
    sons and daughters will be all gentlemen born.

Clown. You are well met, sir. You denied to fight with me
    this other day, because I was no gentleman born. See you
    these clothes? Say you see them not and think me still no
    gentleman born. You were best say these robes are not 125
    gentlemen born. Give me the lie, do, and try whether I
    am not now a gentleman born.

Autolycus. I know you are now, sir, a gentleman born.

Clown. Ay, and have been so any time these four hours.

Shepherd. And so have I, boy. 130

Clown. So you have. But I was a gentleman born before
    my father, for the king's son took me by the hand and
    called me brother; and then the two kings called my
    father brother; and then the prince my brother and the
    princess my sister called my father father; and so we 135
    wept, and there was the first gentleman-like tears that
    ever we shed.

Shepherd. We may live, son, to shed many more.

Clown. Ay, or else 'twere hard luck, being in so preposter-
    ous estate as we are. 140

Autolycus. I humbly beseech you, sir, to pardon me all the
    faults I have committed to your worship and to give me
    your good report to the prince my master.

Shepherd. Prithee, son, do, for we must be gentle now we
    are gentlemen. 145

Clown. Thou wilt amend thy life?

Autolycus. Ay, an it like your good worship.

Clown. Give me thy hand. I will swear to the prince thou
    art as honest a true fellow as any is in Bohemia.

Shepherd. You may say it, but not swear it. 150

---

122 *denied* refused   139–40 *preposterous* (he intends *prosperous*)   147 *an it
like* if it please

Clown. Not swear it, now I am a gentleman? Let boors and
franklins say it, I'll swear it.

Shepherd. How if it be false, son?

Clown. If it be ne'er so false, a true gentleman may swear
155   it in the behalf of his friend. And I'll swear to the prince
thou art a tall fellow of thy hands and that thou wilt not
be drunk; but I know thou art no tall fellow of thy
hands and that thou wilt be drunk. But I'll swear it, and
I would thou wouldst be a tall fellow of thy hands.

160 *Autolycus.* I will prove so, sir, to my power.

Clown. Ay, by any means prove a tall fellow. If I do not
wonder how thou darest venture to be drunk, not being
a tall fellow, trust me not. Hark! The kings and the
princes, our kindred, are going to see the queen's picture.
165   Come, follow us. We'll be thy good masters.   *Exeunt.*

V, iii   *Enter Leontes, Polixenes, Florizel, Perdita, Camillo,
Paulina, Lords, &c.*

Leontes. O grave and good Paulina, the great comfort
That I have had of thee!

Paulina.   What, sovereign sir,
I did not well, I meant well. All my services
You have paid home. But that you have vouchsafed,
5   With your crowned brother and these your contracted
Heirs of your kingdoms, my poor house to visit,
It is a surplus of your grace which never
My life may last to answer.

151 *boors* peasants   152 *franklins* small landowners, farmers   156 *tall . . .
hands* bold fellow, quick to act   164 *picture* (the statue is later said to have
been painted; see V, iii, 47–48, 81–83)   165 *good masters* benefactors
V, iii, 4 *paid home* rewarded handsomely   7 *surplus . . . grace* additional
show of your kindness   8 *answer* repay in kind

Leontes.   O Paulina,
  We honor you with trouble. But we came
  To see the statue of our queen. Your gallery   10
  Have we passed through, not without much content
  In many singularities; but we saw not
  That which my daughter came to look upon,
  The statue of her mother.
Paulina.   As she lived peerless,
  So her dead likeness, I do well believe,   15
  Excels whatever yet you looked upon
  Or hand of man hath done. Therefore I keep it
  Lonely, apart. But here it is. Prepare
  To see the life as lively mocked as ever
  Still sleep mocked death. Behold, and say 'tis well. 20
          Paulina [reveals] Hermione [standing] like a statue.
  I like your silence; it the more shows off
  Your wonder. But yet speak; first, you, my liege.
  Comes it not something near?
Leontes.   Her natural posture!
  Chide me, dear stone, that I may say indeed
  Thou art Hermione; or rather, thou art she   25
  In thy not chiding, for she was as tender
  As infancy and grace. But yet, Paulina,
  Hermione was not so much wrinkled, nothing
  So aged as this seems.
Polixenes.   O, not by much.
Paulina. So much the more our carver's excellence,   30
  Which lets go by some sixteen years and makes her
  As she lived now.
Leontes.   As now she might have done,
  So much to my good comfort, as it is
  Now piercing to my soul. O, thus she stood,

12 *singularities* rarities 19 *lively mocked* vividly imitated

35 Even with such life of majesty — warm life,
    As now it coldly stands— when first I wooed her!
    I am ashamed. Does not the stone rebuke me
    For being more stone than it? O royal piece,
    There's magic in thy majesty, which has
40 My evils conjured to remembrance and
    From thy admiring daughter took the spirits,
    Standing like stone with thee.

Perdita.   And give me leave,
    And do not say 'tis superstition, that
    I kneel and then implore her blessing. Lady,
45 Dear queen, that ended when I but began,
    Give me that hand of yours to kiss.

Paulina.   O, patience!
    The statue is but newly fixed, the color's
    Not dry.

Camillo. My lord, your sorrow was too sore laid on,
50 Which sixteen winters cannot blow away,
    So many summers dry. Scarce any joy
    Did ever so long live; no sorrow
    But killed itself much sooner.

Polixenes.   Dear my brother,
    Let him that was the cause of this have power
55 To take off so much grief from you as he
    Will piece up in himself.

Paulina.   Indeed, my lord,
    If I had thought the sight of my poor image
    Would thus have wrought you — for the stone is
        mine —
    I'ld not have showed it.

Leontes.   Do not draw the curtain.

38 *piece* i.e. piece of sculpture 40 *conjured* summoned 41 *admiring* wondering *spirits* life-giving elements 56 *piece up* make up

Paulina. No longer shall you gaze on't, lest your fancy   60
  May think anon it moves.
Leontes.   Let be, let be.
  Would I were dead, but that, methinks, already —
  What was he that did make it? See, my lord,
  Would you not deem it breathed? and that those veins
  Did verily bear blood?
Polixenes.   Masterly done.   65
  The very life seems warm upon her lip.
Leontes. The fixture of her eye has motion in't,
  As we are mocked with art.
Paulina.   I'll draw the curtain.
  My lord's almost so far transported that
  He'll think anon it lives.
Leontes.   O sweet Paulina,   70
  Make me to think so twenty years together!
  No settled senses of the world can match
  The pleasure of that madness. Let 't alone.
Paulina. I am sorry, sir, I have thus far stirred you; but
  I could afflict you farther.
Leontes.   Do, Paulina,   75
  For this affliction has a taste as sweet
  As any cordial comfort. Still methinks
  There is an air comes from her. What fine chisel
  Could ever yet cut breath? Let no man mock me,
  For I will kiss her.
Paulina.   Good my lord, forbear.   80
  The ruddiness upon her lip is wet;
  You'll mar it if you kiss it, stain your own
  With oily painting. Shall I draw the curtain?
Leontes. No, not these twenty years.

60 *fancy* imagination 67 *fixture . . . in't* the eye, though fixed (stationary),
seems to move 72 *settled* calm, sane

Perdita.   So long could I
Stand by, a looker on.
85 *Paulina.*   Either forbear,
Quit presently the chapel, or resolve you
For more amazement. If you can behold it,
I'll make the statue move indeed, descend
And take you by the hand. But then you'll think —
90 Which I protest against — I am assisted
By wicked powers.
Leontes.   What you can make her do,
I am content to look on; what to speak,
I am content to hear, for 'tis as easy
To make her speak as move.
Paulina.   It is required
95 You do awake your faith. Then all stand still;
Or those that think it is unlawful business
I am about, let them depart.
Leontes.   Proceed.
No foot shall stir.
Paulina.   Music! Awake her, strike!   *[Music.]*
'Tis time; descend; be stone no more; approach;
100 Strike all that look upon with marvel. Come,
I'll fill your grave up. Stir, nay, come away;
Bequeath to death your numbness, for from him
Dear life redeems you. You perceive she stirs.
                         [Hermione comes down.]
Start not; her actions shall be holy as
105 You hear my spell is lawful. Do not shun her
Until you see her die again, for then
You kill her double. Nay, present your hand.

---

86 *presently* at once   *resolve* prepare   96 *Or* (The folio reading *On:* is retained by many editors. Hanmer first suggested *Or.*)   *unlawful* i.e. because of the help of evil spirits   102 *him* death   107 *double* doubly

When she was young you wooed her; now in age
Is she become the suitor?

Leontes.   O, she's warm!
If this be magic, let it be an art   110
Lawful as eating.

Polixenes.   She embraces him.

Camillo. She hangs about his neck.
If she pertain to life, let her speak too.

Polixenes. Ay, and make it manifest where she has
    lived,
Or how stol'n from the dead.

Paulina.   That she is living,   115
Were it but told you, should be hooted at
Like an old tale; but it appears she lives,
Though yet she speak not. Mark a little while.
Please you to interpose, fair madam. Kneel
And pray your mother's blessing. Turn, good lady;   120
Our Perdita is found.

Hermione.   You gods, look down,
And from your sacred vials pour your graces
Upon my daughter's head! Tell me, mine own,
Where hast thou been preserved? where lived? how
    found
Thy father's court? For thou shalt hear that I,   125
Knowing by Paulina that the oracle
Gave hope thou wast in being, have preserved
Myself to see the issue.

Paulina.   There's time enough for that,
Lest they desire upon this push to trouble
Your joys with like relation. Go together,   130
You precious winners all; your exultation

122 *graces* blessings 129 *upon this push* at this point 130 *like relation*
similar account 131–32 *your exultation . . . to* share your joy with

139

Partake to every one. I, an old turtle,
Will wing me to some withered bough and there
My mate, that's never to be found again,
Lament till I am lost.

135 *Leontes.*   O, peace, Paulina!
Thou shouldst a husband take by my consent,
As I by thine a wife. This is a match,
And made between's by vows. Thou hast found mine;
But how, is to be questioned, for I saw her,
140 As I thought, dead, and have in vain said many
A prayer upon her grave. I'll not seek far —
For him, I partly know his mind — to find thee
An honorable husband. Come, Camillo,
And take her by the hand, whose worth and honesty
145 Is richly noted and here justified
By us, a pair of kings. Let's from this place.
What! look upon my brother. Both your pardons,
That e'er I put between your holy looks
My ill suspicion. This your son-in-law
150 And son unto the king, whom heavens directing,
Is troth-plight to your daughter. Good Paulina,
Lead us from hence, where we may leisurely
Each one demand and answer to his part
Performed in this wide gap of time since first
155 We were dissevered. Hastily lead away.   *Exeunt.*

---

132 *turtle* turtledove (a symbol of faithful love and of sadness)   148 *holy*
chaste   155 *dissevered* separated

*Details of the
Pelican Shakespeare and
other Penguin books
follow.*

THE PELICAN SHAKESPEARE

General Editor: Alfred Harbage

Tragedies

Comedies

Histories and Poems

PLAYS BY BERNARD SHAW

*The following plays are published
in Penguin editions. Each play has the
complete text and the
author's preface*

ANDROCLES AND THE LION

THE APPLE CART

ARMS AND THE MAN

BACK TO METHUSELAH

CAESAR AND CLEOPATRA

CANDIDA

THE DEVIL'S DISCIPLE

THE DOCTOR'S DILEMMA

MAJOR BARBARA

MAN AND SUPERMAN

THE MILLIONAIRESS

PLAYS UNPLEASANT

PYGMALION

SAINT JOAN

SEVEN ONE-ACT PLAYS

SELECTED ONE-ACT PLAYS (2 VOLS.)